# MICROWAVE COOKING PROPERLY EXPLAINED

## WITH RECIPES

by
ANNETTE YATES

**PAPERFRONTS**

**ELLIOT RIGHT WAY BOOKS**

**KINGSWOOD, SURREY, U.K.**

*Another Paperfront by Annette Yates*

OUT OF THE FREEZER INTO THE MICROWAVE is
Annette's *combination* book to help make using the two
appliances together as much second nature as using your
hoover. It includes probably the most comprehensive
defrosting guide in print and is packed with a further
selection of mouth-watering easy family-size recipes.

*Uniform with this book.*

Set, printed and bound in Great Britain by
Cox & Wyman Ltd, Reading

# Contents

# Illustrations

# Acknowledgements

The author would like to thank Sharp Electronics (UK) Ltd., Thorpe Road, Newton Heath, Manchester 10, for the use of a microwave oven to test the recipes in this book. Thanks also to TI Creda Ltd., Creda Works, PO Box 5, Blythe Bridge, Stoke-on-Trent, for the loan of an oven for a short period. Finally, I am grateful to Mr. J. G. Davies, M.B.E., Physicist at the Cardiac Department of St. George's Hospital, London, S.W.I. for his helpful advice on the safety of microwave ovens and their possible effect on cardiac pacemakers (page 14).

# Introduction

Microwave cooking is a most efficient method of preparing food and the microwave oven is fast becoming basic kit in the kitchen – particularly for use alongside the home freezer. Reading the following pages you will realise that the microwave oven, by itself, cannot replace the conventional cooker. As with other types of cooking equipment it is used to its best advantage in conjunction with other appliances. The grill, the hob, the conventional oven and the microwave oven work together as a team.

Although you may find it a little difficult to adapt to cooking with microwaves at first and may find yourself falling back on traditional methods to 'save time and effort', do remember that a new cooking technique has to take a while to be mastered. I hope, however, that with this book your microwave oven will be fitting snugly into your lifestyle sooner than expected. Initially it is difficult to believe that foods can possibly cook in such a short time – and without applying any heat. The most common mistake made by newcomers to microwaves is over-cooking. You may well think back to the time you were learning traditional cooking techniques and remember how you made the occasional mistake and learned from it. Similarly with microwave cooking, only experience will tell you what can and cannot be done in your particular oven to suit your personal needs and tastes.

Whether you enjoy cooking, or you spend as little time as possible in the kitchen, a microwave oven can prove indispensable. There are so many benefits. In particular, a microwave oven is cheap to run, simple and clean to use and very, very speedy. A baked potato in its jacket cooks in just four minutes, a 2½lb/1 kg joint of beef in twenty minutes and a baked egg in forty-five seconds.

Cooking by microwaves is an easy and economical way of cooking small quantities too. When cooking for one, for instance, it would be so easy to rely solely on the frying pan.

By using a microwave oven a more varied and balanced diet can be achieved with little extra effort.

Microwave cooking also seems to appeal to all – male and female, young or old and can be a blessing for handicapped people. My husband is very pleased to cook a meal if he can use the microwave oven.

Today the microwave oven is certainly an important part of my life. I enjoy using it, for as well as improving the quality and variety of my diet (and that of my family) it also helps me to organise my increasingly full life more efficiently. I hope this book will encourage you to achieve the same.

Since this book was first published many people have told me how much they enjoy using the recipes (which, I must admit, were the joy of writing the book). Hopefully they will appeal to you too.

A.Y.

# 1

# Advantages

*Speed*
Time is saved since food can be thawed, heated, or cooked in a fraction of the time normally taken. For example, a roast chicken leg takes about four minutes to cook in a microwave oven compared with 20 minutes in a conventional oven, a joint of lamb ($3\frac{1}{2}$ lb/1.6kg) 30 minutes compared with 90 minutes, and a baked apple $2\frac{1}{2}$ instead of 30 minutes.

*Economy*
The energy produced is directed straight into the food. No energy is wasted on heating the cooking container or the oven walls. No pre-heating of the oven is necessary and little heat is lost. The kitchen remains cooler too. The cooking time is short and the amount of fuel actually used is small (a 600W oven uses 1·2Kw of power). A microwave oven uses only about one quarter of the fuel normally consumed by a conventional oven; running costs are low because overall energy consumption can be so drastically reduced. Cooking small quantities (or for one person) is particularly economical. Additionally, time spent in the kitchen may be cut down if wished.

*Versatility*
Defrosting, heating, boiling, baking, roasting and poaching can all be carried out using the same piece of equipment. The microwave oven also speeds up processes such as softening (butter), melting (jelly, chocolate), drying (breadcrumbs, herbs) and dry roasting (nuts). Reheating is straightforward in the microwave oven and produces excellent results.

*Ease of use*
The controls are few and learning how to use them is simple and straightforward. Microwave ovens can be used anywhere there is a 13- or 15-amp socket outlet.

## Convenience

Food can be prepared *when* it is required, so there is no need to plan menus greatly in advance. If a family member is late home a plated meal can be re-heated in minutes. Food usually thawed at room temperature can speedily be defrosted in a microwave oven. Cooking is clean and easy with a microwave oven, and almost anyone can operate one.

Food can be cooked in the serving dish which cuts down on washing up.

The microwave oven can be moved from one room to another or even outdoors.

Oven cleaning is minimal and easy. Since neither the oven interior nor the cooking container is directly heated, foods are not 'baked on'. Microwave cooking is a clean method with fewer kitchen smells. This in turn will result in a cleaner kitchen with less decorating necessary.

Cooking for one person is easy and economical in a microwave oven – no need to heat up a conventional oven just for one person or small amount of food. Small quantities of food (for baby perhaps?) can be cooked, thawed or re-heated easily and hygienically.

Finally, special foods or diets can be less of a chore if you have a microwave oven. Foods cook in their own juices with little need for the addition of fat. So microwave cooking is most suitable for preparing low-fat or fat-free diets.

## Hygiene

The food becomes hot in a very short time, so microwave cooking is an effective way of destroying harmful germs. This is particularly important when reheating food as there is an increased chance of bacteria being present. Microwave cooking is a hygienic method of preparing baby food (take care though; the centre of food prepared in a microwave oven becomes very hot so make sure it is cool enough before serving).

# 2

# Limitations

Browning and crisping is difficult in the majority of microwave ovens because no external heat is applied to the food. As with other cooking appliances, fullest use of the microwave oven can be made if it is operated in conjunction with other forms of cooking – a hob or a grill for instance. Some microwave ovens incorporate a browning element (but they cannot be used while microwave cooking is in progress) or a browning dish. Others have additional elements from which hot air can be forced into the oven. This type may be used as a microwave or a conventional oven. By using both methods foods can be browned before or after the microwave cooking. Turn to page 28 for further information on browning.

Deep fat frying should *never* be attempted in a microwave oven.

Metal utensils should not be used in a microwave oven since they distort the microwave pattern and this can damage the oven. Therefore if you have a large selection of stainless steel, ceramic-coated metal dishes and casseroles, etc., you will need to purchase containers specifically for microwave cooking. China with decorative metal patterns should not be used or the pattern will blacken.

If more than 1 pt/500ml/$2\frac{1}{2}$ cups of water is to be boiled it is quicker and cheaper to use an electric kettle.

Just a few foods are not prepared successfully in a microwave oven. An egg in its shell, for example, will probably explode in the oven. Foods coated with batter are not reheated successfully. The batter becomes soggy. Similarly, fried or roast potatoes heated in a microwave oven will not have their characteristic crisp exterior.

Cakes with a high proportion of dried fruit are not successfully cooked. Cakes containing cream (fresh or butter) will not thaw evenly – the cream will defrost before the cake.

The success of pastry will depend on your taste. Personally

I prefer it cooked conventionally. Unless you have a combination microwave cooker (see page 33) it is not possible to obtain a result similar to that cooked in a conventional oven. It will not be as crisp and it will not brown. However, you may find that the result is acceptable, particularly when cooking flan cases before filling. Do not attempt to cook pies with a top and bottom crust. The filling will bubble out before the pastry cooks.

Bread can be proved most successfully in a microwave oven. It may be cooked using microwaves too but it will not produce a characteristic brown, crisp crust. However, the bread can simply be put into a conventional oven for last minute browning and crisping.

It is not possible to toast bread in a microwave oven.

Microwaves do not tenderize the tougher cuts of meat. Unless your oven has a variable power control (so the power can be reduced, see page 18) it is probably better to cook these cuts conventionally, using long, slow cooking or pressure cooking. Alternatively cooking may be slowed down by using the "defrost" control (see page 24). Cooking times will, obviously, be increased.

Remember dishes can always be thawed and/or reheated in the microwave oven.

Generally those foods requiring gentle cooking are not suitable for microwave cooking. Egg custard is a typical example, though the result will be more successful if the power of your oven can be reduced (see page 18). Soufflés do not cook successfully since there is no external heat to 'set' the crusty exterior which holds its shape.

Cooking some foods in the microwave oven saves little or no time, though it is convenient to cook in the serving dish. For example rice, pasta and some vegetables cook superbly (rice remains separated and fluffy, pasta beautifully firm) but have similar cooking times to conventional methods. You may, therefore, wish to cook these conventionally whilst using the microwave oven for another part of the meal.

# 3

# What is a microwave oven?

*How it works*
Cooking with microwaves is quite different from conventional methods which employ fuels such as gas and electricity. Conventional methods rely on conduction, convection and radiation of heat which has been applied directly to the surface of the food. Microwave cooking does not. The microwave energy is directed on to and penetrates the food. The high frequency energy disturbs the food molecules, generating the heat which cooks it.

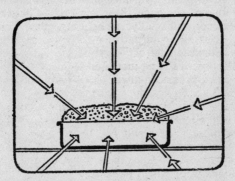

**Fig. I. Food absorbs the microwaves.**

So a microwave oven is one specially designed to control electromagnetic waves (microwaves) directed into it, using them to cook the food. These same waves make possible television, radio, radar and infra-red radiation.

Electric energy is converted by a valve called a magnetron (see page 17) into electromagnetic waves which are then directed into the microwave oven. A stirrer, or paddle, usually in the top of the oven, turns slowly and evenly to help distribute the microwaves uniformly round the oven. Once in the oven, three things can happen to the microwaves. They can be:

(1) *Absorbed* The make up of food and liquid includes many molecules of water. When exposed to microwaves these molecules absorb the energy which causes them to start agitating at an incredible speed (2,450 million times per second). It is this 'excitement' or 'disturbance' of the molecules that produces the heat to cook the food. So heat is created within the food itself. Hence the speed of cooking.

Microwaves can penetrate up to $(1\frac{1}{2}-2$ in) 35–50mm only. However, when cooking a large joint for example, the heat generated in this area (all round and above and below the joint) is sufficient to cook the centre. The outer heat is conducted to the centre.

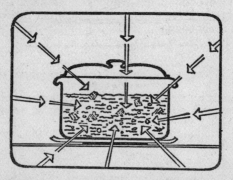

**Fig. 2. Certain containers transmit microwaves.**

(2) *Transmitted* Microwaves pass straight through some materials. These include glass, china, wood, and some paper and plastics. Since these materials contain little or no water, they do not absorb the microwaves. This type of material therefore is ideal for containers for food to be cooked by microwaves. The container does not heat up but the food inside does. If the food container becomes hot it is because heat is being conducted from the food.

(3) *Reflected* Metal reflects microwaves. They are, for instance, reflected off the sides, base and roof of the oven, so that the food absorbs microwaves from all directions. For this reason cooking utensils and containers which include metal should not be used in a microwave oven unless the manufacturer specifically recommends it on certain occasions (covering small areas of food with foil to protect it,

for example). They will reflect the microwaves, preventing the food from cooking.

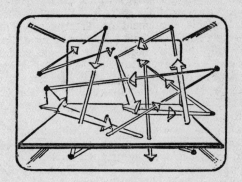

**Fig. 3. The metal walls of the oven reflect the microwaves.**
(Food is not shown in the oven for the purposes of the diagram. Remember it should never be switched on while empty).

*Safety Features*

Firstly, do remember that microwaves are similar to radio waves and should not be confused with X-rays. Microwaves are non-ionizing and cause a change in temperature only, *not* a chemical change as in ionizing rays such as gamma rays and X-rays.

Safety standards in Britain dictate stringent rules on safety devices, permissible microwave leakage from ovens, and the maintenance of the equipment within these leakage limits during the life of the oven. For example, leakage at (2 in) 5cm away from any part of the oven is limited to 5mW/sq cm. As the distance from the oven is increased, so the leakage decreases. At arm's length it would have decreased to 0·005mW/sq cm.

The presence of the **BEAB** label for household appliances (British Electrotechnical Approvals Board) means that the microwave oven has met safety requirements dictated by the relevant British Standard Specification for electrical safety and microwave leakage limits.

**Fig. 4. BEAB label.**

All microwave ovens are fitted with automatic cut-outs which come into operation when the door is opened (even a fraction) and when cooking time is completed.

Each microwave oven is tested before it leaves the factory. After this it should be checked or serviced about every twelve months by a manufacturer's authorized engineer. He will do this in your home and will test the level of leakage using a special meter. Please read pages 31/32 about caring for your oven.

Should you wish to have your oven checked, contact your dealer, manufacturer or appointed contractor. Some local council environmental health departments will also carry out checks.

*Note:* Heart Pacemakers

Microwave ovens which are well maintained are perfectly safe (as explained in detail on page 32). However, a few early types of cardiac pacemaker *may* be susceptible to interference when in close proximity to electro-magnetic fields such as those caused by microwave ovens and, incidentally, by some electric razors. If in doubt do not hesitate to seek medical advice.

*Construction*
Please refer to Fig. 5.

1. Lead from oven to 13 amp plug.
2. Door fastening. Ovens vary with the type of door fastening. Some are on the door itself, some have a button or switch on the control panel, some are fixed in the door handle, and some have no latch as such. Microwave oven

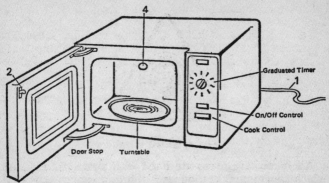

**Fig. 5. General construction of a microwave oven.**

doors are electrically sealed. They have two or three switches ensuring that energy is automatically switched off as soon as the door is opened even a fraction. It will not start again until the 'cook' control is operated.

3. Shelf or turntable. The food is raised off the floor of the oven by a special type of glass shelf. This shelf is removable and, if broken, should never be replaced with any glass or plastic shelf other than that of the proper specification. The shelf has three functions: (*a*) it positions the food in the oven to best advantage – so that the food absorbs power evenly from all directions; (*b*) it makes the job of mopping up any spilled food easier; (*c*) it helps to protect the magnetron (the energy generator) from its own microwaves should the empty oven be switched on accidentally.

4. Interior light. This usually lights as soon as the oven is switched on at the mains. Some ovens have a separate switch, while some light up only when the oven is 'cooking'.

5. Controls. There are usually three basic controls: an 'on/off' control, a timer control, and a 'cook' control. The 'on/off' control, as well as switching on the oven, usually switches on a cooler fan and an interior light. With a few ovens it is necessary to wait for about 10 seconds to allow the power source to warm up before use. Some ovens do not have this control and are brought into operation simply by connection to the mains. The timer control is

usually graduated into minutes but they will vary in the maximum cooking time from oven to oven. On average it is 20–30 minutes. Below 10 minutes the timer is usually graduated into 10 or 15 and/or 30 second divisions. The 'cook' control switches on the microwave energy within the oven cavity.

6. Door stop.

Additionally some microwave ovens include the following:

- Indicator lights – to remind the cook that an operation has been set, is in progress, or has finished.
- Audible reminders – a bell or buzzer indicating that the cooking process has ended.
- Automatic defrost – when thawing frozen foods it is necessary to rest the food after a short period of exposure to the microwave energy. Some ovens have a control which does this automatically (see page 24).
- Rotating table – food cooked in a microwave oven needs to be turned and/or stirred to ensure even heating. Some ovens incorporate a turntable which automatically takes the food through all the wave patterns to produce even cooking. Some models now incorporate an alternative to the turntable. This consists of specially positioned stirrers (paddles or antennae) usually beneath the floor or in the roof of the oven cavity. The function of these stirrers is to achieve good distribution of the microwave energy throughout the oven and ensure even cooking. The cleaning of this type of oven is simplest of all – just wipe over the empty cavity walls.
- Variable microwave output – many of the latest models offer a choice of microwave output. This means that the cooking rate can be altered to suit the food being cooked. For example: High/full power, roast, reheat, medium, simmer, defrost, keep warm, low, etc. (see also page 18).
- Browning dish or skillet – some manufacturers supply a special dish or plate made of material which does absorb and is heated by microwaves. The empty dish is preheated to a high temperature and food placed on the dish is browned or seared (see pages 22 and 28). During microwave cooking the food is turned over to brown the other side. Follow manufacturers' instructions carefully for the use and care of these dishes.
- Browning element – this is a built-in element enabling foods to be browned in the microwave oven before or

after they have been cooked. It cannot be used while the microwave cooking is taking place.

● Touch controls – these are built into the front panel. Just a touch on the appropriate panel will begin the cooking process – with no switches, buttons or dials. Touch controls are easy to keep clean.

● Microwave thermometer (or temperature probe/sensor or meat probe) – this is inserted into a joint of meat for example and will show when the correct temperature has been reached – a convenient way of ensuring the meat is cooked to the preferred "doneness". *When buying a meat probe make sure it is suitable for use in a microwave oven.* Some ovens have a probe fixed inside. The cook sets it to the correct temperature and the oven automatically switches itself off at the end of cooking.

● Shelf – this means two layers of food can be cooked. Cooking time will be longer, because the microwave energy has to be shared between the extra quantities of food. The shelf is usually removeable and generally food on the lower level tends to cook more slowly (so foods with shorter cooking times should be positioned here).

● Hot air convection – hot air is forced from hot elements into the oven. Foods are browned by convection either before or after microwave cooking. It is also possible to use the oven conventionally.

● Memory controls – these enable the cook to pre-set microwave cooking power level and times. For example, the oven may be set to switch on at a specific time, cook the food and switch off at, or keep the food warm until, a pre-set time. Some models incorporate programme cards which are simply fed into the controls and the oven does the rest.

● Trolley – some manufacturers offer a portable trolley to move the microwave oven round.

Please refer to Fig. 6 on page 19.

1. The *Power Transformer* converts the 240 voltage to a very high voltage suitable for use by the magnetron.

2. The *Magnetron* alters this very high voltage to a very high frequency voltage, thus generating microwaves (electro-magnetic waves of 2,450MHz). This part of the oven is often called the 'heart' of the oven and usually carries a

long guarantee.
3. The *Waveguide* directs the microwave energy from the magnetron to the oven cavity.
4. The *Wave Stirrer* or *Paddle* consists of slowly revolving metal blades. These distribute the microwaves round the oven.
5. The *Oven* has metal walls which deflect the microwaves, directing them into the food. The transparent door panel and its surround are fitted with specially designed seals which ensure that microwaves do not escape from the oven. A metal grill inside the glass (which is denser than the microwaves) makes sure no energy passes out. The door is also fitted with an automatic cut-out which operates when the door is opened.

*Oven Power*
Microwave ovens vary in the power output from model to model. The higher the oven wattage (power output) the faster the cooking. The recipes in this book were prepared using a 600W oven. Some models incorporate a variable power output. These work exactly the same as fixed power models but the power level can be altered. So the speed of cooking can be controlled. For example the power may be lowered for cooking egg custard or tough cuts of meat which prefer longer, slower cooking; and raised for roasting meat. Many models include settings such as: low, keep warm, defrost, simmer, medium, bake, roast, reheat, high/full power. Follow manufacturer's instructions for their correct use.

# 4

## Installation

A microwave oven can be positioned almost anywhere. All it needs is a convenient 13- or 15-amp socket. Place it on a work surface, on a table, or on a trolley so that it may be moved from one room to another or even out of doors. A microwave oven is not a large piece of equipment and since it creates few cooking smells and little steam it is suitable for use anywhere.

Always follow your manufacturer's instructions carefully and never try to repair a fault yourself (see pages 31 and 32).

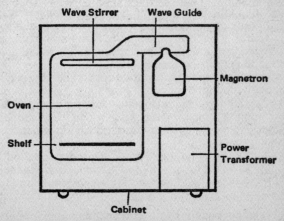

**Fig. 6. Working parts of a microwave oven.**

# 5

# Containers and Utensils

Most non-metal containers can be used in a microwave oven. The container must allow the microwaves to pass straight through into the food. If in doubt as to whether a container is suitable for microwave cookery, check with the manufacturers' instruction book or with the manufacturer of the container.

*Never* use metal containers, and if your instruction book suggests the use of foil for protecting small parts of food, make sure that it does not touch the oven walls. Any container which heats up while the food remains cool is not suitable for use.

The following materials may be used in a microwave oven:

*China, glass ceramic, and oven-to-table glass* can be used for most cooking operations. Do not however use containers with a decorative metal design since this will ruin both the microwave pattern in the oven and the metal design on the container (it will spark and blacken).

*Plastics.* Some plastic containers can be used for heating food in a microwave oven, though cooking in them is usually not possible. Freezer-to-microwave containers are very useful. They can withstand cooking and freezing temperatures within a specific range. Follow manufacturer's instructions for their correct use.

Most plastics are only suitable for short heating periods or they will scorch.

Highly coloured foods (tomato sauce for example) tend to stain some plastic containers in which they are heated.

Plastic foam plates should be used for short periods only or they may melt.

Cooking cling film may be used for covering food being heated or cooked in the microwave oven. Roasting bags and boil-in bags are also useful (always remember to pierce these to allow steam to escape).

*Glass* can be used for short-term heating but do not attempt to use cut glass and thick glass which is liable to crack.

*Paper plates, towels and napkins* are suitable for supporting or covering food in the microwave oven. Greaseproof paper and kitchen paper are also useful for this purpose. *Do not use paper in a microwave oven which has a browning element.*

*Wood* can be used to hold food while it is heated. There is a certain amount of water in wood so it does warm up a little. For this reason it is not a good idea to leave a wooden spoon in a sauce for example, while it is cooking.

*Straw baskets and platters* are suitable for holding food, such, as bread, which is to be heated in the microwave oven.

*Cotton or linen napkins* can be used to wrap or support food which is to be heated (bread for example).

*Microwave containers* of various shapes and sizes are offered by independent manufacturers as well as manufacturers of microwave ovens. Always follow instructions carefully for their use.

**N.B.** Containers which have been repaired with glue or have glued handles, etc., should not be used in a microwave oven – the glue may melt.

*The Shape of the Container*
The shape of the container will affect the cooking time of the food. Experience will tell you which of your containers will best suit a particular food. The following points are helpful to encourage even cooking!
1. Try to use containers of a regular shape – a round dish instead of an oval dish, for example.
2. Spread food pieces over a large shallow dish rather than a deep one.
3. A container with straight sides will transmit microwaves more evenly than one with curved sides.
4. When thawing foods, the frozen block should fit the container as closely as possible. If the thawing food or liquid is allowed to spread over a large dish it will over-heat before the remaining food is defrosted.

*A Cover for the Container*
When heating or cooking foods where the moisture is to be retained, a cover should be used: e.g. soups, casseroles, vegetables.

Casserole lids, plates (check the list of suitable materials on page 20 for guidance on which to use), and cling film can be used to cover food. Always remove the lid carefully at the end of cooking – remember there will be steam trapped beneath.

Cover foods which normally tend to spit, e.g. chops, bacon, baked beans.

Dry foods such as bread, cake and pastry do not need to be covered.

### Accessories

A wide range of specially-designed microwave accessories and cookware is readily available. Here are just a few useful items.

*Roasting racks* raise meats and poultry above their cooking juices. Made of tough plastic or ceramic, they are also suitable for reheating dry foods such as bread and pastry.

*Plate rings/covers* are used for stacking plates of food which are to be thawed and/or reheated. For even results no more than two plates should be stacked at one time.

*Browning dishes or skillets* are ideal for most foods which are conventionally grilled or fried, e.g. chops, bacon, sausages, beefburgers, fish fingers, potato cakes, chicken pieces, mushrooms. See also pages 16 and 28.

*Microwave thermometer* details on page 16.

# 6

# Using the Microwave Oven

The microwave oven can be used to thaw, heat or cook food. It is only necessary to calculate the cooking *time* in relation to the amount of food being prepared. Cooking temperatures are not applicable when cooking with microwaves. It is worth remembering though that the following points will affect the timing:

1. *The type of food* – its moisture content (the more moisture it contains the longer it will take) and its density (dense foods such as meat will take longer than porous foods such as bread or cake).
2. *The quantity of food* – two chops will take longer than one (though not necessarily twice the time). Avoid filling the microwave oven with food. It is quicker, and therefore more economical, to heat or cook small amounts.
3. *Its shape and thickness* A regular shape will cook more evenly. It is a good idea therefore to bone and roll irregular shaped joints of meat. Thinner pieces of food cook faster than thick ones. Large pieces of food should be cut into smaller pieces when appropriate to allow the microwaves to penetrate them faster. These small pieces should also be of even thickness.
4. *Its starting temperature* Food from the refrigerator will take slightly longer to cook than food at room temperature.
5. *The container used* particularly its shape. A regular shape with straight sides is best (see page 21).
6. *The arrangement of the food* If meat slices or pieces of fish are piled up in a cooking container they will cook unevenly. Make sure they are evenly distributed in the container. When putting cooked meals on a plate for reheating later, make sure the arrangement is even (no high piles of potatoes for example).

*Turning and stirring*
Turning and stirring food in the microwave oven assists even cooking. This is when a microwave oven with a turn-

table is particularly advantageous. The food is automatically rotated through the wave patterns so there are no hot and cold spots in the food. Remember to place the food off centre on the turntable. Never position food so there is a circle of small items with one in the centre. The one in the centre will tend not to cook. Details of the latest alternative to a turntable appear on page 16.

## Standing time

When cooking is completed and food is removed from the microwave oven it will in fact go on cooking for a short period. The heat generated in the food is sufficient to cook it after it comes out of the oven. Joints of meat for instance will go on producing heat and conducting it to the centre for 15 to 30 minutes after removal from the microwave oven. To undercook therefore is a good rule. If the food is not cooked to your taste after a short standing period (or carry-over time) it is a simple matter to put it back into the microwave oven for a few seconds or minutes longer.

## Thawing

If you own a freezer, then a microwave oven is its ideal companion. Food can be defrosted in minutes instead of hours. So it is not necessary to decide at 7 a.m. what you would like to eat at 7 p.m.; and no need to panic at the arrival of unexpected guests. Food may be taken from the freezer when required and be ready for serving in a matter of minutes.

Microwaves speed up the normal process of thawing food. But be warned. The microwaves melt the smallest ice crystals first. Should the food then be subjected to a continuous period of microwave energy, the melted parts could begin to heat up while the larger crystals remained frozen. The result would be food which was hot and frozen in the same container. To avoid this the microwaves should be applied to the frozen food gently or in 'bursts' with rests between. The rest periods allow the larger crystals to start melting. The heat from the thawed areas is conducted to the frozen areas. This process can be done manually, switching the oven on and off to incorporate cooking and rest periods. Rest periods should be of at least two minutes for joints of meat and whole poultry and one minute for smaller meat pieces or poultry portions.

Most microwave ovens have an automatic 'defrost'

control which switches the oven on and off (once the required time has been selected), for example, 30 seconds on followed by 30 seconds off. This ensures even thawing. Thawing time depends on the food and the quantity being defrosted.

The automatic defrost system can also be used for slower cooking, of casseroles for instance, or delicate mixtures such as cakes or bread. Your manufacturer's instruction book will give guidance on this.

It is advisable to allow the food to stand for about 10 minutes after removing it from the microwave oven to be sure that all the ice crystals have melted. The food can then be prepared and/or cooked in the normal way.

Some foods can be cooked directly from the frozen state (vegetables for example). Others, such as fish, can be cooked from a partially frozen state. Joints of meat and poultry should be completely thawed before cooking if best results are to be obtained.

*Points to remember when thawing food:*
- Keep food covered during thawing, except baked foods such as bread and cakes.
- Keep turning or rotating the food during defrosting. This is done automatically if your oven has a turntable or alternative stirrer (paddles or antennae). When thawing items such as chicken portions it will be necessary to rearrange them once during defrosting to encourage even thawing.
- A frozen block of food should fit its container as closely as possible so that the defrosting food does not spread out and overheat before the rest of the food is defrosted.
- Always remove any large lumps of ice off foods to be thawed (vegetables for example). Ice slows down the defrosting process.
- When thawing liquids, such as soups, speed up the operation by breaking up the partially frozen food with a fork or spoon, and stirring occasionally.
- It is better to thaw some foods partially and then allow them to stand in room temperature to continue thawing. Fruit or raw pastry, for example, could easily begin to cook if subjected to microwaves for too long.
- A meat thermometer may be used on a large joint of meat to determine if the interior is still frozen. *Do not* however leave the thermometer in the microwave oven while it is

switched on, unless it is one specifically designed for this use.

● Small pieces of food such as fish fillets, cup cakes, pastries, leftovers, etc., do not need rest periods during thawing. These can be subjected to a short continuous period of thawing.

● Commercially frozen foods can be thawed in a microwave oven. Since many such foods are packed in foil dishes it is necessary to decant them into suitable containers first. Many frozen food manufacturers label their packets to indicate whether they are suitable for microwave heating and give other relevant instructions.

The following chart may be used as a guide to thawing times. Slight adjustments may need to be made according to the shape of the food and its density.

| Food | Thawing time |
| --- | --- |
| Meat joint (3 lb/1·4kg) | 15 mins (turn over after 10 mins) plus 15–20 mins standing time |
| Chicken (3 lb/1·4kg) whole | 12 mins (turn over after 10 mins) plus 15–20 mins standing time |
| Chicken portions (4) | 6–8 mins (separate after 3 mins) plus 10 mins standing time |
| Minced beef (1 lb/500g) | 6 mins (turn over after 3 mins) plus 10 mins standing time |
| Chops (2 lb/900g) | 10 mins (separate after 6 mins) plus 10 mins standing time |
| Steaks (1 lb/500g) ¾ in/1½cm thick | 6 mins (separate after 4 mins) plus 10 mins standing time |
| Fish fillets (1 lb/500g) | 2 mins. Do not thaw completely |
| Plated meal (thawing and heating) | 7–10 mins |
| Cooked meat dishes or soup, casseroles, etc. (1 lb/500g) | 10 mins approx (stir to break it up during thawing) |

| | |
|---|---|
| Rice, cooked (8 oz/225g) | 4–5 mins (stir during thawing) plus 2 mins standing time |
| Fruit: e.g. strawberries, raspberries, apple slices (1 lb/500g) | 5–8 mins (stir gently during thawing). Do not thaw completely |
| Bread: loaf | 3 mins plus 5 mins standing time |
| slice | 15–30 secs |
| roll | 15–30 secs |
| Cake (8 in/20cm) | 3 mins plus 5 mins standing time |
| Cup or fairy cake (1) | 30 secs plus 2 mins standing time |
| Biscuit (1) | 15 secs |

*Reheating*

Reheating of pre-prepared and pre-plated meals is simple in a microwave oven. No need to worry if a member of the family arrives home late to a cold meal. The result is also more successful than reheating by conventional methods. A conventional oven needs pre-heating before allowing the radiant heat to be conducted slowly to the centre of the food. Even then the outer surfaces tend to dry out by the time the centre is heated. No need to pre-heat the oven when re-heating with microwaves. The food is heated through very quickly, retaining most of its moisture content and so there is no drying up on the edges. Additionally the very speedy heating throughout the food means that bacteria and germs have far less chance to survive. It is therefore a safer method of reheating. This is particularly important when preparing food for a baby.

Plated meals can be kept for a latecomer or they may be frozen for reheating in a few days or weeks. In either case the food is very quickly and evenly reheated (about 3–4 minutes from room temperature or 7–10 minutes from frozen). The result is a most appealing meal presented in its original state. Even after freezing, thawing and reheating, most of the water content is retained so the food looks and tastes as it did when it was laid out on the plate.

Even heating of a plated meal depends on the thickness and shape of the food and the way it is arranged. Vegetables etc., should be of uniform shape and size and the food generally laid evenly over the plate. This simple rule of even arrangement will ensure even heating.

Some microwave ovens have a browning element which is useful for browning reheated dishes. The element cannot be used while microwave cooking itself is taking place.

*Browning food*

Any meat or poultry which is cooked in a microwave oven will brown naturally to a degree, without aid. However, the microwaves themselves do not brown food. So foods which require browning in order to appeal to the eye and taste buds (meat particularly) need extra treatment. The grill or frying pan may be used to brown the meat initially, then it can be speedily cooked through in the microwave oven. Often, not only does this add to the colour of the finished dish but also to the flavour. Roasting bags also help produce an acceptable colour on roasts, particularly chicken.

Some ovens have a browning dish which is suitable for use *only* in a microwave oven. This dish is usually made of a thermal ceramic. It is pre-heated in the microwave oven (the time depends on what is to be cooked) then the food is placed on the dish and seared and browned to produce the traditional effect. During microwave cooking the food is turned over so that the other side is browned. Remember to handle these dishes with care. They can become very, *very* hot. Always use oven gloves and protect your work surface with a wooden board, or similar cover, before placing the hot dish down. Always follow manufacturer's instructions for the use of these dishes.

Other models have a browning element which may be used after (but *not* during) microwaving or they incorporate hot air convection with which you can do your browning either before or after the microwave cooking. See pages 9, 16 and 17.

# 7

# Meal Planning

Meal planning can be quick and simple using a microwave oven. When first using a microwave oven you may find that meals need a little more planning time than those you usually cook conventionally. Do not be disheartened; like other things, experience will prove a great asset. You will soon appreciate that the time saving is worth the extra planning. Another advantage is that meals can be prepared several hours in advance so avoiding any last minute panic. Foods reheated in a microwave oven do not lose their fresh taste and colour; they do not dry up. So it is a good idea to undercook slightly foods to be served during the meal; and simply reheat them when required.

For example, to prepare the following menu:
  Tomato Soup, page 39
  Beef with Horseradish page 68
  Parsley Baked Onions, page 99
  Baked Potatoes (savoury), page 105
  Plum and Walnut Compote, page 113

Prepare and cook in advance the Tomato Soup, Baked Potatoes and Plum and Walnut Compote. Prepare the ingredients for the Parsley Baked Onions. About 1 hour before serving time, cook the Beef with Horseradish. While the beef is standing, cook the Parsley Baked Onions and reheat the potatoes. Prepare the sauce for the beef (keeping the beef warm if you do not wish to reheat it in the microwave oven before serving). Reheat the soup in the serving dishes and serve. Reheat any of the main course if necessary just before taking it to the table. Slices of meat can be reheated on the plates. Reheat the Plum and Walnut Compote just before taking it to the table.

Here I have demonstrated how to get three hot courses to the table at one meal. At first glance it may seem complicated but you will soon find that you do not need to think and pre-plan quite so carefully. It helps of course, as with meals cooked conventionally, to include a cold starter or dessert, which can be prepared in advance.

Foods requiring very short cooking can be cooked in the microwave oven while other foods are being served, and advantage can be taken of the time when meat joints etc. are being defrosted in the microwave oven to prepare ingredients for other dishes.

Do not be *too* determined to cook *everything* in the microwave oven. Great savings can still be made in time and effort if you plan your meals using the microwave oven in conjunction with your other cooking appliances. For example, you may wish to cook the main food in the microwave oven while preparing a quick sauce on the hob (particularly if the sauce is to be poured over the food before serving).

# 8

# Care of the Microwave Oven

Before cleaning remember to disconnect the microwave oven from the electricity supply. Microwave cooking is a clean method of cooking. Generally, food is covered so there is little splashing and the walls do not heat up. However, when splashes do occur they should be wiped off the oven walls immediately with a damp cloth. It is pointless to waste microwave energy on cooking spilled food. An easy method of cleaning the oven interior is to boil a container of water in the oven for about 2 minutes. The resulting condensation may be wiped from the surfaces with a soft dry cloth.

Similarly removable bases and glass or plastic shelves or turntables should be cleaned frequently. Should any of these be broken, do not replace it with anything other than a replacement supplied by the manufacturer.

Always clean the oven interior after use, to ensure efficient cooking during the next operation. Keep the oven cavity, door and seals clean by using mild detergent in water. Some strongly flavoured foods may cause the oven to have an odour (as with conventional methods sometimes). This odour can be removed by boiling some water and lemon juice in a dish in the microwave oven for a few minutes. When necessary wipe the oven exterior with a damp cloth. Avoid splashing water over vents.

Never use abrasives or steel wool to clean a microwave oven – a scratch on the oven wall may distort the carefully-designed wave pattern. Follow manufacturers' instructions for use of commercial cleaners.

Never use a knife to clean off a stubborn mark.

Do not operate the oven without food inside. If there is nothing in the oven to absorb the microwaves when it is switched on, the oven can be severely damaged. Keep a cup of water in the oven when it is not in use in case someone accidentally switches it on.

Do not use metal containers in the microwave oven.

Do not use containers with a decorative metal design. The design will spark and blacken when exposed to microwaves.

Do not use aluminium foil in the microwave oven unless the manufacturer specifically states this is possible (for protecting chicken wing tips from drying out, for example).

Never hang a cloth on or dry tea-towels on, the door. Never lean heavily on the door.

The air filter and splatter guard (over the wave stirrer) should be checked frequently and cleaned. Always follow your manufacturer's instructions. Generally they should be washed in warm, soapy water, rinsed, dried and fitted back into the oven.

Always obtain qualified help if a fault occurs. Do not attempt to repair the oven yourself. Should the oven be damaged (perhaps by dropping it or knocking it while moving) do not use it. Do not use the oven if the door has been damaged obviously. Call your dealer, manufacturer or appointed contractor.

Remember that, as with any other appliance, respectful, careful handling, always following manufacturers' instructions, will ensure a long and efficient life.

Every microwave oven is tested for leakage levels when it leaves the factory to make sure it meets British Standard requirements (see page 14). Have the oven tested or serviced regularly, once a year, by a manufacturer's authorized engineer. He will measure the level of leakage using a special meter. This is usually carried out as part of a regular servicing in your home. If the oven is well maintained, regularly serviced, and manufacturer's instructions are carefully followed, your microwave oven is safe. If you have any doubts, have the oven checked.

Some manufacturers offer a home servicing contract which involves regular checking of the oven.

# 9
# Choosing a Microwave Oven

Choosing a microwave oven should be done with as much care as choosing any other major piece of kitchen equipment. Perhaps it is for a family, a young couple, an elderly person, a bedsitter, or even a sickroom. No matter which, the advantages are numerous (see page 7). Your choice of oven will depend on the type of cooking you will be doing. Here is a list of questions to guide you.

Does the microwave oven carry a guarantee? Look for a longer guarantee for the magnetron. This is usually more than one year and up to five years. Does the manufacturer offer a service contract?

Does the oven carry a safety label such as the BEAB label? See page 14.

How much space do you have for a microwave oven? Check the measurements. How much space does the manufacturer recommend you leave around the oven? Do you want it to sit on the kitchen worktop? Do you wish to move it from room to room?
    Are you completely re-fitting your kitchen? If so, you may wish to choose a double-oven microwave cooker or a combination microwave cooker. Double-oven microwave cookers are available as free-standing cookers or as two-level built-in appliances. Often the microwave oven is situated above the conventional oven; the grill is usually positioned in the oven and the hob sits above or is separate. Combination microwave cookers offer sheer convenience, though are currently most expensive. Microwave and conventional cooking takes place in the same oven cavity.

Do you have a freezer? If so it is a good idea to choose an oven which has an automatic defrost control. See page 24.

Would a variable power microwave oven be of advantage to you? It is helpful if you often cook the tougher cuts of meat, or delicate puddings such as egg custard for example, which need long slow cooking. See page 18.

Do you have an efficient grill? If not you may want to choose a model which incorporates a browning element, a browning dish, or hot air convection.

Are you prepared to stand by and turn food in the oven (to assist even cooking)? You will probably prefer a model incorporating an automatic turntable or its alternative (see page 16). I strongly recommend choosing one of these.

Will most of your containers, plates, etc., fit easily into your chosen oven or will you need to purchase special dishes? Remember too that those with a clear floor (i.e. no turntable) will hold larger, angular containers.

Does the oven have indicator lights or audible reminders to draw your attention to the fact that microwave cooking/ thawing is taking place, finished, etc.?

Look at the controls and see which you prefer: buttons, slides, dials, touch controls, etc.?

Which type of door opening do you prefer? Some models incorporate doors which slide up. These are of advantage if your space is particularly limited. Others have side-opening, or drop-down doors.

Is the instruction book clear and comprehensive? Are the recipes easy to follow?

# 10

## About the Recipes

The recipes in the following pages were created using a microwave oven with a power output of 600W and a turntable fitted. The cooking times may vary slightly according to the power of your oven. The higher the wattage, the faster the cooking.

All cooking takes place in the microwave oven except when mentioned.

Quantities are usually for 4 or 6 people – the number is given at the beginning of each recipe. Remember that the cooking time will need to be altered if you alter the quantity to be cooked. For convenience, the cooking time (period that the microwave oven is in use) is also given at the beginning of each recipe.

The method of freezing is given at the end of the recipe. If it is not suitable for freezing, no instruction is given.

When food requires covering during cooking, instruction is given in the method. Similarly, if the cooked dish requires a carry-over or standing period, this is also mentioned (see page 24).

If your microwave oven does not have an automatic turntable or alternative (see page 16) it will be necessary to turn or stir the food in some of the recipes which follow. It is usually a simple matter of turning the dish around in the oven a quarter or a half. Experience will serve as your best guide on how much turning is necessary. Your instruction book will also give you the appropriate advice for your particular model.

Ingredients are given in imperial (Imp.), metric (Met.) and American (Am.) quantities. It is advisable to follow one type of measure. Where accuracy is important exact equivalents are given. Otherwise, figures have been rounded off to convenient measures. Tin sizes vary considerably. When the ingredients list a can of food, the weights quoted on the label (usually exact equivalents) are given.

All spoon quantities are level unless otherwise stated.

The following tables will be useful for converting your own recipes. The figures are not exact equivalents but rounded-up, convenient measures.

*Capacity*

| Imperial | Metric | American |
|---|---|---|
| $\frac{1}{4}$ pt | 150ml | $\frac{2}{3}$ cup |
| $\frac{1}{2}$ pt | 300ml | $1\frac{1}{4}$ cups |
| $\frac{3}{4}$ pt | 400ml | 2 cups |
| 1 pt | 500–600ml | $2\frac{1}{2}$ cups |
| $1\frac{1}{2}$ pt | 900ml | $3\frac{3}{4}$ cups |
| $1\frac{3}{4}$ pt | 1 litre | $4\frac{1}{4}$ cups |
| 2 pt | 1·1 litre | 5 cups |

N.B.  British pint     =20 fl oz          1 tsp  =5ml
         American pint=16 fl oz          1 tbsp =15ml

*Weight*

| Imperial | Metric |
|---|---|
| $\frac{1}{2}$ oz | 15g |
| 1 oz | 25g |
| 2 oz | 50g |
| 3 oz | 75g |
| 4 oz | 100–125g |
| 5 oz | 150g |
| 6 oz | 175g |
| 7 oz | 200g |
| 8 oz | 225g |
| 9 oz | 250g |
| 10 oz | 275g |
| 12 oz | 350g |
| 14 oz | 400g |
| 16 oz/1 lb | 450g |
| $1\frac{1}{2}$ lb | 700g |
| 2 lb | 900g |
| 3 lb | 1·4kg |
| 5 lb | 2·3kg |

**1 American cup:**
Flour 4 oz/100g
Fats 8 oz/225g
Dried fruit 5 oz/150g
Sugar 8 oz/225g

1 oz/25g Sugar=2 tbsp
1 oz/25g Butter=2 tbsp
1 oz/25g Flour=$\frac{1}{4}$ cup

# SOUPS & STARTERS

It is a speedy job to make your own fresh soup in a micro-wave oven – either individual portions, or large quantities. A good tasty stock, prepared from broken-up bones, a chicken carcass, or vegetable leftovers (including washed peelings), can be made in about 30 minutes and used as a basis for a soup or a stew. So soups prepared in a micro-wave oven can prove a most economical venture, in terms of time spent in the kitchen, ingredients, and the amount of fuel used. Hopefully the soups in the following pages will give you ideas for experimenting with your own recipes. Canned soups can be heated and dried soups can be re-constituted in a microwave oven.

In this section you will find several recipes for starters that are simply prepared with the assistance of a microwave oven. Gelatine can be dissolved in a few minutes without the bother of a bowl over a pan of hot water. Butter is melted in two minutes – for Potted Salmon.

*Tips for Soup Making*

Use a deep container rather than a shallow one.

Use a container large enough to hold the soup without it boiling over, particularly those where milk is an ingredient. Stirring the soup occasionally ensures even distribution of heat and therefore even cooking with a smooth result. This is particularly important if your oven does not have an automatic turntable.

Take care not to overheat soup containing eggs or cream.

When converting your own recipes for microwave cooking, you may need to increase the quantity of liquid slightly to allow for evaporation.

Fresh soups are prepared conventionally by long, slow cooking to help develop the flavour. The flavour of micro-wave-cooked soup can be improved further by allowing it to stand for some time after cooking. It is a simple matter to reheat the soup before serving.

When reheating soups, best results are obtained when individual portions of soup are heated in serving bowls or mugs.

Always stir the soup well before serving.

*Canned soups*: Empty the soup into a suitable container and stir well before heating. An individual portion in a bowl takes about 2 minutes.

*Dried soups*: Mix the powder with hot water before heating in the microwave oven. 1½ pt/900ml/3¾ cups takes about 4–6 minutes. Allow the soup to stand for 5–10 minutes before serving. Reheat in the microwave oven if necessary.

*Freezing and Thawing Soups*

Do not add egg or cream to soups which are to be frozen and then defrosted in a microwave oven. They should be added just before serving (remember not to overheat though, or the egg or cream will separate).

Thawing time will depend on the amount and type of soup. Break up the soup with a fork and stir well as it defrosts.

Soups prepared with less liquid take up less room in the freezer. Extra liquid can always be added to the concentrated soups before reheating.

## Tomato Soup

| *Servings:* 4–6 | *Cooking time:* 25 mins | | |
|---|---|---|---|
| | Imp. | Met. | Am. |
| Butter | 1 oz | 25g | 2 tbsp |
| Bacon rasher (slice), finely chopped | 1 | 1 | 1 |
| Onions, finely chopped | 8 oz | 225g | ½ lb |
| Carrots, finely chopped | 4 oz | 100g | ¼ lb |
| Tomatoes, skinned and chopped | 1 lb | 450g | 1 lb |
| Chicken stock, hot | ¾ pt | 400ml | 2 cups |
| Salt and black pepper | | | |
| Bouquet garni | 1 | 1 | 1 |
| Sugar | 2 tsp | 2 tsp | 2 tsp |
| Lemon juice | 2 tsp | 10ml | 2 tsp |
| Tomato purée (paste) | 2 tbsp | 2 tbsp | 2 tbsp |

*Method*

Place the butter, bacon, onions and carrots in a suitable deep casserole. Cover and cook for 5 minutes. Stir in the remaining ingredients and cook for 20 minutes, stirring once. Allow the soup to stand for 15 minutes then remove bouquet garni. Liquidize the soup before serving with croûtons and chopped parsley.

*Freezing:* Pour into a freezer-to-microwave or polythene container, cool, cover, label and freeze.

*Variations*: For Cream of Tomato Soup stir in ¼ pt (150ml/
⅔ cup) single (thin) cream before serving.

This soup may also be prepared using canned tomatoes
(14 oz/397g/medium) instead of fresh tomatoes.

## French Onion Soup

| *Servings:* 4–6 | *Cooking time:* 15mins + 1½ mins | | |
|---|---|---|---|
| | *Imp.* | *Met.* | *Am.* |
| Butter | 2 oz | 50g | 4 tbsp |
| Onions, cut into thin rings | 1 lb | 450g | 1 lb |
| Beef stock, hot | 1 pt | 500ml | 2½ cups |
| Salt and pepper | | | |
| Worcestershire sauce | 1 tbsp | 15ml | 1 tbsp |
| Cheese, grated | 3 oz | 75g | 3 oz |
| French bread, thick slices | 4 | 4 | 4 |

*Method*
Place the butter and onions into a suitable deep casserole,
cover and cook for 5 minutes. Add the stock, seasoning to
taste and Worcestershire sauce. Cover and cook for 10
minutes, stirring once. Allow to stand for 15 minutes before
serving.

Meanwhile, spread the cheese on one side of each slice of
bread. Arrange them on a plate, cook (uncovered) for 1½
minutes and then float them on top of the soup to serve.

*Freezing*: Do not include the bread and cheese. Pour into a
freezer-to-microwave or polythene container, cool, cover,
label and freeze.

*Variation*: To make Cream of Onion Soup, liquidize the
soup and stir in ¼ pt (150ml/⅔ cup) single (thin) cream.
Sprinkle over some fried onion rings to serve.

## Butter Bean Soup

| *Servings:* 4–6 | | *Cooking time:* 25 mins | |
|---|---|---|---|
| | *Imp.* | *Met.* | *Am.* |
| Butter beans | 8 oz | 225g | ½ lb |
| Bicarbonate of soda (baking soda) | 1 tsp | 1 tsp | 1 tsp |

| | Imp. | Met. | Am. |
|---|---|---|---|
| **Butter** | 1 oz | 25g | 2 tbsp |
| **Onions, chopped** | 8 oz | 225g | ½ lb |
| **Streaky bacon, chopped** | 2 oz | 50g | 2 oz |
| **Chicken stock, hot** | 1 pt | 500ml | 2½ cups |
| **Mixed herbs** | ½ tsp | ½ tsp | ½ tsp |
| **Salt and pepper** | | | |
| **Single (thin) cream** | ¼ pt | 150ml | ⅔ cup |
| **Parsley, chopped** | 1 tbsp | 1 tbsp | 1 tbsp |

*Method*
Soak the butter beans overnight in plenty of water with the bicarbonate of soda (baking soda).

Place the butter, onions, and bacon into a suitable deep casserole, cover and cook for 5 minutes, stirring once. Add the drained butter beans and the chicken stock, herbs and seasoning and cook for 20 minutes, stirring once.

Allow the soup to stand for 15 minutes then stir in the cream and sprinkle over the chopped parsley before serving.

*Freezing:* Omit cream and parsley. Pour into a freezer-to-microwave or polythene container, cool, cover, label and freeze.

## Potato and Courgette Soup

*Servings:* 4–6          *Cooking time:* 23 *mins*

| | Imp. | Met. | Am. |
|---|---|---|---|
| **Margarine** | 1 oz | 25g | 2 tbsp |
| **Onions, chopped** | 8 oz | 225g | ½ lb |
| **Potatoes, diced** | 1 lb | 450g | 1 lb |
| **Courgettes (squash), sliced thinly** | 8 oz | 225g | ½ lb |
| **Chicken stock** | 1 pt | 500ml | 2½ cups |
| **Bay leaf** | 1 | 1 | 1 |
| **Salt and pepper** | | | |

*Method*
Place the margarine and onions into a suitable deep container and cook, uncovered, for 3 minutes. Stir in the potatoes and courgettes. Cover and cook for 10 minutes. Add the remaining ingredients (not too much salt) cover and cook

for 10 minutes. Allow to stand for 15 minutes before serving with crusty bread. Remove bay leaf before serving.

*Freezing*: Pour into a freezer-to-microwave or polythene container, cool, cover, label and freeze.

*Variation:* For a creamier soup liquidize and stir in $\frac{1}{4}$ pt (150ml/$\frac{2}{3}$ cup) single (thin) cream before serving.

## Chicken and Vegetable Broth

*Servings:* 4  *Cooking time:* 40 *mins*

|  | Imp. | Met. | Am. |
|---|---|---|---|
| Chicken portion (quarter) | 1 | 1 | 1 |
| Water | $\frac{1}{2}$ pt | 300ml | 1$\frac{1}{4}$ cups |
| Bay leaf | 1 | 1 | 1 |
| Bouquet garni | 1 | 1 | 1 |
| Salt and pepper | | | |
| Turnip, diced | 4 oz | 100g | $\frac{1}{4}$ lb |
| Carrots, diced | 8 oz | 225g | $\frac{1}{2}$ lb |
| Onion, chopped | 4 oz | 100g | $\frac{1}{4}$ lb |
| Worcestershire sauce | 2 tbsp | 30ml | 2 tbsp |
| Water | $\frac{1}{4}$ pt | 150ml | $\frac{2}{3}$ cup |

### Method
Place the chicken, water, bay leaf and bouquet garni into a suitable casserole, cover and cook for 20 minutes. Allow to stand for 10–15 minutes then strain the mixture. Skin and chop the chicken into small pieces. Place the chicken pieces, strained stock, seasoning to taste and the remaining ingredients into a large suitable casserole. Cover and cook for 20 minutes. Allow to stand for 15 minutes before serving with hot crusty bread or croûtons.

*Freezing:* Pour into a freezer-to-microwave or polythene container, cool, cover, label and freeze.

# Beef and Vegetable Soup

*Servings:* 4                           *Cooking time: 35 mins*

|  | Imp. | Met. | Am. |
|---|---|---|---|
| Cooking oil | 1 tbsp | 15ml | 1 tbsp |
| Stewing beef, cut into very small pieces | 6 oz | 175g | 6 oz |
| Onions, chopped | 8 oz | 225g | ½ lb |
| Carrots, chopped | 4 oz | 100g | ¼ lb |
| Leek, chopped | 1 | 1 | 1 |
| Beef stock, hot | 1½ pt | 1 litre | 3¾ cups |
| Tomato purée (paste) | 2 tbsp | 2 tbsp | 2 tbsp |
| Mixed herbs | ½ tsp | ½ tsp | ½ tsp |
| Salt and pepper | | | |

*Method*
Place the cooking oil, chopped beef, onions, carrots and leek into a large suitable container. Cover and cook for 5 minutes, stirring once. Add the remaining ingredients, cover and cook for 30 minutes, stirring once. Allow the soup to stand for 15–20 minutes before serving with hot crusty bread.

*Freezing:* Pour into freezer-to-microwave or polythene container, cool, cover, label and freeze.

# Spiced Fruit Soup

*Servings:* 4                           *Cooking time: 20 mins*

|  | Imp. | Met. | Am. |
|---|---|---|---|
| Pears, peeled, cored and sliced | 1 lb | 450g | 1 lb |
| Juice of orange | 1 | 1 | 1 |
| Dry cider | ¾ pt | 400ml | 2 cups |
| Mixed spice | ½ tsp | ½ tsp | ½ tsp |
| Cloves | 2 | 2 | 2 |
| Mint to garnish | | | |

*Method*
Place all the ingredients except mint, into a deep suitable casserole. Cover and cook for 20 minutes, stirring once.

Allow the soup to stand for 10–15 minutes then remove the cloves and liquidize. Chill well before serving. Garnish each bowl of soup with a sprig of mint.

*Freezing:* Pour into a freezer-to-microwave or polythene container, cool, cover, label and freeze.

*Variations:* Other fruits may be substituted for pears, e.g. apples (peeled and cored), plums (peeled and stoned) or a mixture. Try using different spices too, e.g. nutmeg, cinnamon.

## Egg in a Pot

| *Servings:* 1 | | *Cooking time:* 1¾ *mins* | |
|---|---|---|---|
| | *Imp.* | *Met.* | *Am.* |
| Streaky bacon rasher (slice), chopped | 1 | 1 | 1 |
| Butter | ½ oz | 15g | 1 tbsp |
| Egg | 1 | 1 | 1 |
| Salt and pepper | | | |
| Slice of tomato | 1 | 1 | 1 |
| Cheese, grated | 1 tbsp | 1 tbsp | 1 tbsp |

### Method
Place the bacon and butter in a suitable small pot or ramekin dish. Cover and cook for 1 minute. Stir well. Break the egg on to the bacon, season to taste and top with the tomato slice and grated cheese. Cook uncovered for 45 seconds. Allow to stand for ½–1 minute before serving with triangles of thin toast.

## Garlic Mushroom Starter

| *Servings:* 4 | | *Cooking time:* 4–5 *mins* | |
|---|---|---|---|
| | *Imp.* | *Met.* | *Am.* |
| Butter | 2 oz | 50g | 4 tbsp |
| Garlic clove, crushed | 1 | 1 | 1 |
| Button mushrooms, wiped and trimmed | 8 oz | 225g | ½ lb |
| Salt and black pepper | | | |
| Parsley, chopped | 2 tbsp | 2 tbsp | 2 tbsp |

*Method*
Place the butter and garlic into a suitable deep container.
Cook for 1 minute or until melted and foaming. Add the
mushrooms and stir well until coated with butter. Season
with salt and black pepper. Cover and cook for 3–4 minutes,
stirring at least once. Stir in the parsley before serving with
triangles of hot toast.

*Variation:* The garlic may be replaced with 1 tsp or more of
your favourite herb.

## Hot Grapefruit with Sherry

*Servings:* 4           *Cooking time: 5 mins*

| | Imp. | Met. | Am. |
| --- | --- | --- | --- |
| Grapefruit, halved | 2 | 2 | 2 |
| Sherry | 4 tsp | 20ml | 4 tsp |
| Demerara sugar | 8 tsp | 8 tsp | 8 tsp |
| Butter | ½ oz | 15g | 1 tbsp |

*Method*
Using a grapefruit knife or a small sharp knife, cut around
each segment until they are all loosened. Place the grapefruit halves into suitable serving dishes. Pour 1 tsp sherry on
each grapefruit half, then sprinkle 2 tsp of sugar over each
and place a knob of butter in the centre of each. Cook uncovered for 5 minutes. Serve hot.

## Potted Salmon

*Servings:* 4–6           *Cooking time: 2 mins*

| | Imp. | Met. | Am. |
| --- | --- | --- | --- |
| Can red or pink salmon | 7½ oz | 213g | medium |
| Lemon juice | 1 tbsp | 15ml | 1 tbsp |
| Tabasco sauce | 1 drop | 1 drop | 1 drop |
| Salt and pepper | | | |
| Butter | 4 oz | 100g | ¼ lb |
| To garnish: | | | |
| Lemon slices | | | |
| Cress | | | |

*Method*
Drain the salmon, remove bones and skin and flake roughly with a fork. Stir in the lemon juice, Tabasco sauce and seasoning to taste. Place the butter in a suitable container and cook for 2 minutes to melt. Mix the salmon into the melted butter, pour into 4 small pots and allow to set. Turn out before serving and garnish with lemon slices and cress. Serve with toast triangles.

*Freezing:* Freeze in the pots.

*Variations:* Replace the salmon with shrimps, drained flaked tuna, or drained mashed sardines.

## Ham and Parsley Vol-au-Vents

| *Servings:* 4 | | *Cooking time:* 4 mins | |
|---|---|---|---|
| | *Imp.* | *Met.* | *Am.* |
| Butter | 1 oz | 25g | 2 tbsp |
| Flour | 1 oz | 25g | ¼ cup |
| Milk | ½ pt | 300ml | 1¼ cups |
| Cayenne pepper | ¼ tsp | ¼ tsp | ¼ tsp |
| Salt | | | |
| Ham, cooked, chopped | 4 oz | 100g | ¼ lb |
| Parsley, chopped | 2 tbsp | 2 tbsp | 2 tbsp |
| Small vol-au-vent cases, cooked | 8 | 8 | 8 |

*Method*
Place the butter in a suitable bowl or jug and cook for 30 seconds to melt. Stir in the flour then gradually add the milk, stirring continuously. Cook for 3 minutes, stirring every minute. Add the cayenne pepper and season with salt. Stir in the ham and parsley. Heat the vol-au-vent cases for about 1 minute then pile in the ham mixture. Serve immediately.

If they are to be served later, do not heat the empty cases. Pile the mixture into the vol-au-vent cases then reheat in the microwave oven for 2–3 minutes before serving.

*Freezing:* Freeze cases and filling separately.

*Variations:* Replace the ham with any cooked, flaked fish.

# Tomato Mould

*Servings:* 4–6                              *Cooking time:* 3 mins

|  | Imp. | Met. | Am. |
|---|---|---|---|
| Tomato juice | ¾ pt | 400ml | 2 cups |
| Powdered gelatine | ½ oz | 15g | 1 pkt |
| Tabasco sauce | 2 drops | 2 drops | 2 drops |
| Salt and pepper |  |  |  |
| To garnish: |  |  |  |
| Watercress |  |  |  |
| Tomato wedges |  |  |  |

*Method*

Place half the tomato juice in a suitable bowl or jug and sprinkle over the gelatine, stirring well. Cook for 3 minutes to dissolve, stirring every minute. Add the remaining tomato juice, Tabasco sauce and seasoning to taste. Pour into a ring mould and refrigerate to set. To serve, turn out on to a serving dish and fill the centre with watercress. Garnish with tomato wedges.

# Tomato Starter

*Servings:* 4                                *Cooking time:* 5–6 mins

|  | Imp. | Met. | Am. |
|---|---|---|---|
| Large tomatoes, halved | 4 | 4 | 4 |
| Cheese, grated finely | 2 oz | 50g | 2 oz |
| French mustard | 2–4 tsp | 2–4 tsp | 2–4 tsp |
| Worcestershire sauce | 1 tsp | 5ml | 1 tsp |
| Black pepper |  |  |  |
| Toasted breadcrumbs | 2 tbsp | 2 tbsp | 2 tbsp |

*Method*

Arrange the tomato halves round the edge of a suitable plate. Mix together the cheese, mustard, Worcestershire sauce and black pepper to taste. Spread a little of the mixture on top of each tomato half. Cook for 5–6 minutes, removing any tomato that is cooked. Sprinkle the toasted breadcrumbs over each tomato and serve immediately.

## Liver Pâté

*Servings:* 4                                  *Cooking time:* 20 *mins*

|                            | Imp. | Met. | Am. |
|----------------------------|------|------|-----|
| Lambs' liver               | 6 oz | 175g | 6 oz |
| Bacon                      | 3 oz | 75g  | 3 oz |
| Onion                      | 1 oz | 25g  | 2 tbsp |
| Garlic clove, crushed      | 1    | 1    | 1 |
| Butter                     | 1 oz | 25g  | 2 tbsp |
| Flour                      | 1 oz | 25g  | 2 tbsp |
| Milk                       | ½ pt | 300ml | 1¼ cups |
| Salt                       | 1 tsp | 1 tsp | 1 tsp |
| Black pepper               | ½ tsp | ½ tsp | ½ tsp |
| Bay leaves                 | 4    | 4    | 4 |

*Method*

Mince the liver, bacon and onion twice (or put into a powerful blender). Stir in the garlic. Place the butter in a suitable container or jug and cook for 1 minute to melt. Stir in the flour then gradually add the milk, stirring well. Season with salt and black pepper. Cook for 4 minutes, stirring every minute, until the sauce is thick. Pour the sauce over the liver and mix together well. Pour the pâté into four small pots. Place a bay leaf on top of each. Put the pots into a suitable large container and pour boiling water round to come halfway up their sides. Cook uncovered for 15 minutes. Allow to cool then chill before removing bay leaves and serving with triangles of thin toast.

*Freezing:* Freeze in the pots, cover with foil, label and freeze.

## Pizza Topping

*Servings:* 6–8   *Coats 2 pizza bases 8 in/20cm diameter*
*Cooking time:* 10 *mins* (topping) 4½ *mins* (pizza)

|                            | Imp. | Met. | Am. |
|----------------------------|------|------|-----|
| Onions, chopped            | 8 oz | 225g | ½ lb |
| Garlic clove, crushed      | 1    | 1    | 1 |
| Streaky bacon, chopped     | 4 oz | 100g | ¼ lb |
| Red pepper, deseeded and chopped | 1 | 1 | 1 |

**Salt and black pepper**

| Butter | ½ oz | 15g | 1 tbsp |
|---|---|---|---|
| Cooking oil | 1 tbsp | 15ml | 1 tbsp |
| Mushrooms, sliced | 4 oz | 100g | ¼ lb |
| Oregano | 3 tsp | 3 tsp | 3 tsp |
| Tomato purée (paste) | 5 tbsp | 5 tbsp | 5 tbsp |

*Method*

Place the first seven ingredients in a suitable deep container, cover and cook for 5 minutes, stirring once. Add the mushrooms, oregano and tomato purée. Cover and cook for a further 5 minutes. Allow to stand for 10 minutes before using.

*Freezing:* Pour the mixture into a freezer-to-microwave or polythene container, cool, cover, label and freeze.

*To prepare pizza:* Use bread dough or a scone mixture for the base, each weighing about 8 oz/225g/½ lb. Allow the bread dough to rise for about 30 minutes (or 20 minutes after 30 seconds heating in the microwave oven – covered with a piece of polythene brushed with cooking oil). Cook the dough in the microwave oven for about 3 minutes. Spread half the topping on one round of dough and cook in the microwave for 1 minute. Sprinkle over some finely grated cheese and cook for a further 30 seconds until the cheese melts. Alternatively, brown the top under a hot grill.

*Freezing:* Place the pizza on a sheet of foil, cool and freeze. Wrap and label when frozen.

# 12

# FISH

The flavour and texture of fish prepared in a microwave oven can be far superior to that prepared conventionally. All the juices are retained. It is cooked simply and quickly, and with fewer of the 'fishy' smells normally associated with conventional methods. The outer surface of the fish does not become dry. It may be cooked whole, stuffed, filleted, or cut into cubes as a casserole. Try making your favourite sauce in the microwave oven then adding the fish fillets and cooking for a further 3–4 minutes.

Shellfish are ideal for microwave cooking. They can be cooked in their shells or as part of a recipe.

Canned fish is simply reheated in the microwave oven,

(decanted into a suitable container) with no loss of flavour.
Serve it with instant mashed potato for a quick meal.
  Here are some guidelines for cooking fish.

*Tips for cooking fish*
Brushing the skin of the fish with a little melted butter improves flavour and prevents it drying out.

Cover fish during cooking and standing time to ensure maximum retention of juices. (Fish coated in breadcrumbs however, or with a commercially prepared coating should not be covered during microwave cooking.)

Whole fish with the skins intact should be slit in a few places to allow steam to escape.

Position the thicker parts of the fish towards the outer edge of the dish. When cooking thin fillets or large whole fish, prevent overcooking by overlapping the thinner tail ends. Remember to turn the container during microwave cooking if your oven does not incorporate a turntable.

When cooking fish as a separate course of a meal, it is a good idea to prepare it at the last minute to avoid overcooking. The vegetables and other courses may always be cooked in advance and reheated just before serving.

It is easy to overcook fish no matter which cooking method you are using, so take extra care not to overcook fish in the microwave oven. It is cooked perfectly when it is easily flaked with a fork. It is better to underestimate the cooking time slightly since the fish will go on cooking after it is removed from the oven. The following times may be used as a guide.

|  |  |
|---|---|
| Fish fingers (2) | about 2 minutes |
| Fish 1 lb/450g | about 3 minutes |
| Fish in sauce 1 lb/450g | about 4 minutes |

The cooked fish should be allowed to stand covered for 5–10 minutes before serving to make sure that the centre is cooked.

*Thawing Fish*
Fish fillets are thawed in seconds. Since fish defrosts so quickly it is better to subject it to short bursts of energy with

rests between (easy if your oven has an automatic defrost button). This ensures that the fish does not start to cook in parts.

Cover the fish and turn it over once during defrosting if it is a large piece.

Partially thawed pieces may be separated under cold running water.

Do not overheat the frozen fish or the outer areas will cook.

To defrost shrimps, prawns, etc., place in a covered container and shake well during the thawing period.

## Plaice in Lemon Sauce

*Servings:* 2                                       *Cooking time:* 5½ *mins*

|                          | Imp.   | Met.  | Am.    |
|--------------------------|--------|-------|--------|
| Butter                   | 1 oz   | 25g   | 2 tbsp |
| Parsley, chopped         | 2 tbsp | 2 tbsp| 2 tbsp |
| Plaice fillets, skinned  | 4      | 4     | 4      |
| Salt and black pepper    |        |       |        |
| Sauce:                   |        |       |        |
| Cornflour (cornstarch)   | 2 tsp  | 2 tsp | 2 tsp  |
| Juice and rind of lemon  | ½      | ½     | ½      |
| Water                    | 3 tbsp | 45ml  | 3 tbsp |

*Method*

Mix together the butter and parsley and spread over the skinned side of the plaice fillets. Roll up the fillets, thick end inside and place in a suitable container. Season with salt and black pepper, cover and cook for 4 minutes. Allow to stand for 5 minutes.

Meanwhile, in a suitable deep bowl or jug, mix together the cornflour, lemon juice and water. Season with salt and black pepper. Cook for 1½ minutes, stirring twice. Pour the sauce over the fish and reheat for ½-1 minute if necessary.

*Variation:* Orange juice and rind can be substituted for lemon in this recipe.

## Buttered Trout

| *Servings:* 4 | | | *Cooking time:* 7 *mins* |
| | *Imp.* | *Met.* | *Am.* |
| Trout, cleaned, heads off | 4 | 4 | 4 |
| Salt and black pepper | | | |
| Butter | 2 oz | 50g | 4 tbsp |
| Spring onions, chopped | 2 tbsp | 2 tbsp | 2 tbsp |
| Parsley, chopped | 2 tbsp | 2 tbsp | 2 tbsp |
| To garnish: | | | |
| Lemon wedges | | | |
| Cress | | | |

*Method*
Season the trout inside and out. Arrange the fish round the outer edge of a large plate. Overlap the tail ends so that there is a more even thickness of fish. Place a quarter of the butter on each trout and sprinkle over the chopped onions and parsley. Cover and cook for 7 minutes giving the plate a quarter turn half-way. Allow to stand covered for 5–10 minutes before serving. If necessary, reheat for 1–2 minutes. Garnish with lemon wedges and cress.

## Smoked Haddock and Spinach

| *Servings:* 4 | | | *Cooking time:* 10 *mins* |
| | *Imp.* | *Met.* | *Am.* |
| Frozen leaf spinach | 1 lb | 450g | 1 lb |
| Red pepper, deseeded and chopped | 1 | 1 | 1 |
| Salt and pepper | | | |
| Flour | 2 tsp | 2 tsp | 2 tsp |
| Top of the Milk | 1 tbsp | 15ml | 1 tbsp |
| Butter | 1 oz | 25g | 2 tbsp |
| Smoked haddock, cut into 4 pieces | 1¼ lb | 575g | 1¼ lb |
| Black pepper | | | |

*Method*
Defrost the spinach. In a suitable container, mix together the spinach and red pepper, seasoning to taste. Mix together the

flour and milk to form a smooth paste and stir into the spinach. Dot with the butter, cover and cook for 5 minutes, stirring once. Allow to stand while the haddock is being cooked.

Place the haddock pieces in a suitable shallow container, sprinkle with black pepper and dot with a little butter if liked. Cover and cook for 4–5 minutes depending on the thickness of the fish.

Arrange the fish on top of the bed of spinach and serve. Delicious as a starter or main meal.

## Fish with Yoghurt Dressing

*Servings:* 4

*Cooking time:* 8 mins

| | Imp. | Met. | Am. |
|---|---|---|---|
| Cod fillets | 1¼ lb | 575g | 1¼ lb |
| Salt and pepper | | | |
| Lemon juice | 1 tbsp | 15ml | 1 tbsp |
| Butter | ½ oz | 15g | 1 tbsp |
| Carton unsweetened yoghurt | 5 oz | 150g | 5 oz |
| Cucumber, diced | 4 oz | 100g | ¼ lb |
| Green grapes, deseeded and halved | 2 oz | 50g | 2 oz |
| Mushrooms, sliced | 2 oz | 50g | 2 oz |

*Method*
Place the cod fillets in a suitable shallow container. Sprinkle with salt and pepper and lemon juice, and dot with the butter. Cover and cook for 5 minutes. Allow to stand for 5 minutes.

Meanwhile mix together the yoghurt, cucumber, grapes and mushrooms with a little seasoning. Pour this mixture over the fish, cover and cook for a further 3 minutes. Allow to stand for 5 minutes before serving.

## Salmon Savoury Ring

*Servings:* 4                          *Cooking time:* 6½ *mins*

|  | Imp. | Met. | Am. |
|---|---|---|---|
| Butter | 1 oz | 25g | 2 tbsp |
| Flour | 1 oz | 25g | ¼ cup |
| White wine | 6 tbsp | 90ml | 6 tbsp |
| Salt and pepper |  |  |  |
| Can salmon | 7½ oz | 213g | medium |
| Eggs, separated | 2 | 2 | 2 |
| Single (thin) cream | 2 tbsp | 30ml | 2 tbsp |

*Method*

Place the butter in a suitable deep container and melt for ½ minute. Stir in the flour and cook for 1 minute. Carefully stir in the white wine and seasoning and cook for 1 minute, stirring once.

Flake the salmon, removing skin, bones and juice. Stir into the sauce. Stir in the lightly beaten egg yolks and cream. Whisk the egg white until light and fluffy then fold into the fish mixture.

Pour into a suitable greased (oiled) ring mould and cook for 5 minutes. Best served hot with slices of hot buttered toast as a starter or it can be served cold with salad as a starter or main meal.

## Prawn Savoury

*Servings:* 4                          *Cooking time:* 10 *mins*

|  | Imp. | Met. | Am. |
|---|---|---|---|
| Butter | 1 oz | 25g | 2 tbsp |
| Large onion, chopped finely | 1 | 1 | 1 |
| Green pepper, deseeded and chopped finely | 1 | 1 | 1 |
| Celery stick (stalk), chopped | 1 | 1 | 1 |
| Cornflour (cornstarch) | 2 tbsp | 2 tbsp | 2 tbsp |
| Can tomatoes, roughly chopped including juice | 14 oz | 397g | medium |

## Prawn Savoury—contd.

| | | | |
|---|---|---|---|
| Sugar | 1 tsp | 1 tsp | 1 tsp |
| Pinch mixed herbs | | | |
| Salt and black pepper | | | |
| Small prawns | 12 oz | 350g | $\frac{3}{4}$ lb |

*Method*

Place the butter, onion, pepper and celery in a suitable container, cover and cook for 3 minutes. Stir in the cornflour then add the tomatoes, sugar, herbs and seasoning. Cover and cook for 4 minutes. Stir in the prawns, cover again and cook for a further 3 minutes. Allow to stand covered for 5 minutes before adjusting the seasoning and serving on a bed of hot rice.

# 13

# Sauces

When cooking sauces in a microwave oven there is no problem of overcooking or burning. White sauce is simply prepared in the serving jug and sauces which require the infusion of herbs, onion, etc., in milk, are easy to prepare in the microwave oven. If ever you have been worried about making Hollandaise sauce – using a double boiler and whisking until that crucial moment – you will find the sauce on page 59 simplicity itself. It can even be reheated in the microwave oven without separating.

Cooked sauces can be quickly reheated and frozen sauces can be thawed and reheated.

*Tips for cooking sauces*
Stir the sauce often during cooking (even if your oven has a turntable) then stir well after cooking.

Cooking times will depend on the sauce, the type of container used, and the starting temperature of the ingredients.

Take care not to overcook sauces containing egg yolks. These will require stirring more frequently to prevent the outer edges from separating.

Use a container large enough to hold the sauce without it boiling over.

Sauces are usually cooked uncovered. However I have found covering to be advantageous in some of the recipes that follow. The method states when to cover.

*Thawing sauces*
Thaw sauces in a covered container. The time taken will depend on the amount and type of sauce being prepared. As the sauce defrosts, help it along by breaking it up with a fork and stirring well as it becomes warmer.

## Tomato Sauce

| *Servings:* 4 | | | *Cooking time:* 10 *mins* |
|---|---|---|---|
| | *Imp.* | *Met.* | *Am.* |
| Butter | ½ oz | 15g | 1 tbsp |
| Cooking oil | 1 tbsp | 15ml | 1 tbsp |
| Medium onion, chopped | 1 | 1 | 1 |
| Flour | 1 tbsp | 1 tbsp | 1 tbsp |
| Can tomatoes, roughly chopped, including juice | 14 oz | 397g | medium |
| Mixed herbs | 1–2 tsp | 1–2 tsp | 1–2 tsp |
| Salt and black pepper | | | |

*Method*
Place the butter, cooking oil and onion, into a suitable container. Cover and cook for 3 minutes. Stir in the flour then add the remaining ingredients. Cover and cook for 7 minutes, stirring twice. Serve with meat, fish or vegetables.

*Freezing:* Pour into a freezer-to-microwave or polythene container, cool, cover, label and freeze.

## White Sauce (pouring)

| *Servings:* 4–6 | | | *Cooking time:* 7 *mins* |
|---|---|---|---|
| | *Imp.* | *Met.* | *Am.* |
| Butter | 1 oz | 25g | 2 tbsp |
| Flour | 1 oz | 25g | 3 tbsp |
| Salt and pepper | | | |
| Milk | 1 pt | 500ml | 2½ cups |

*Method*
Place the butter in a suitable bowl or jug. Cook for 1 minute to melt. Stir in the flour and salt then gradually add the milk, stirring continuously. Cook uncovered for 7 minutes, stirring frequently. Serve with bacon, fish or vegetables.

*Freezing:* Pour the sauce into a freezer-to-microwave or polythene container, cool, cover, label and freeze.

*Variations:* Flavour the sauce with grated cheese, chopped parsley, dried herbs, nutmeg or prawns.

For a coating sauce: use 2 oz/50g/4 tbsp of butter and 2 oz/50g/6tbsp flour.

For a binding sauce: use 4 oz/100g/½ cup of butter and 4 oz/100g/1 cup flour (this is a very thick sauce used for binding croquettes, etc.).

## Bread Sauce

| *Servings:* 4–6 | | *Cooking time:* 5 mins | |
|---|---|---|---|
| | *Imp.* | *Met.* | *Am.* |
| Small onion, quartered | 1 | 1 | 1 |
| Bay leaf | 1 | 1 | 1 |
| Black peppercorns | 6 | 6 | 6 |
| Cloves | 2 | 2 | 2 |
| Milk | ½ pt | 300ml | 1¼ cups |
| Breadcrumbs | 2 oz | 50g | 1 cup |
| Butter | 1 oz | 25g | 2 tbsp |
| Salt | | | |

*Method*
Place the first five ingredients into a deep suitable container. Cook for 3 minutes or until the milk boils. Cover and allow to stand (to infuse) for 1 minute. Strain the mixture and return the milk to the container. Stir in the breadcrumbs and butter, cover and cook for 2 minutes. Season to taste with salt and stir well. Allow to stand for at least 10 minutes before serving. Reheat if necessary. Serve with chicken, turkey or pheasant.

*Freezing:* Place in a freezer-to-microwave or polythene container, cool, cover, label and freeze.

## Hollandaise

| *Servings:* 4 | | *Cooking time:* 2¼ mins | |
|---|---|---|---|
| | *Imp.* | *Met.* | *Am.* |
| Butter | 4 oz | 100g | ½ cup |
| White wine vinegar | 2 tbsp | 30ml | 2 tbsp |
| Dry mustard | ½ tsp | ½ tsp | ½ tsp |
| Salt and pepper | | | |
| Egg yolks, beaten | 2 | 2 | 2 |

*Method*

Place the butter, vinegar, mustard and seasoning into a suitable deep container. Heat for 1½ minutes. Gradually beat in the egg yolks then whisk until creamy (about 2 minutes). Cook for 45 seconds and whisk the sauce again. If the sauce is not yet thick enough cook for a further 15 seconds and whisk again. Continue until thick enough but take care not to overcook or the sauce will separate. Serve with baked fish such as salmon, or vegetables such as asparagus.

## Curry Sauce

*Servings:* 4                                   *Cooking time:* 9 mins

|  | Imp. | Met. | Am. |
|---|---|---|---|
| Cooking oil | 1 tbsp | 15ml | 1 tbsp |
| Onions, chopped finely | 8 oz | 225g | ½ lb |
| Cornflour (cornstarch) | 1 tbsp | 1 tbsp | 1 tbsp |
| Curry paste | 2–3 tbsp | 2–3 tbsp | 2–3 tbsp |
| Can tomatoes, chopped, including juice | 14 oz | 397g | medium |
| Stock (bouillon) | ½ pt | 300ml | 1¼ cups |
| Lemon juice | 2 tbsp | 30ml | 2 tbsp |
| Sugar | 2 tsp | 2 tsp | 2 tsp |
| Salt and black pepper | | | |

*Method*

Place the cooking oil and onions in a suitable container, cover and cook for 3 minutes. Stir in the cornflour then add the remaining ingredients. Cover and cook for 6 minutes, stirring twice.

Serve with cooked meat, poultry or fish on a bed of hot rice.

See below for easy-cook poppadums.

*Freezing:* Pour into a freezer-to-microwave or polythene container, cool, cover, label and freeze.

## Poppadums

Brush both sides of a poppadum with cooking oil and place on a sheet of greaseproof paper. Cook for 1 minute. Drain on

kitchen paper before serving with curry. Two poppadums
take about 1½ minutes.

## Bolognese Sauce

| | Imp. | Met. | Am. |
|---|---|---|---|
| *Servings:* 4 | | *Cooking time:* | 15 *mins* |
| Minced (ground) beef | 1 lb | 450g | 1 lb |
| Onions, chopped | 8 oz | 225g | ½ lb |
| Garlic clove, crushed | 1 | 1 | 1 |
| Can tomatoes, roughly chopped, including juice | 14 oz | 397g | medium |
| Tomato purée | 2 tbsp | 2 tbsp | 2 tbsp |
| Sugar | 1 tsp | 1 tsp | 1 tsp |
| Oregano | 1 tsp | 1 tsp | 1 tsp |
| Basil | ½ tsp | ½ tsp | ½ tsp |
| Black pepper | ½ tsp | ½ tsp | ½ tsp |
| Salt | | | |

*Method*
Place the beef, onions and garlic into a suitable deep container and mix together well. Cover and cook for 5 minutes, stirring twice. Add the remaining ingredients and stir well. Cover and cook for 10 minutes, stirring twice. Allow to stand for 15 minutes before serving with spaghetti, and a little Parmesan cheese.

*Freezing:* Pour into a freezer-to-microwave or polythene container, cool, cover, label and freeze.

## Apple Sauce

| | Imp. | Met. | Am. |
|---|---|---|---|
| *Servings:* 4–6 | | *Cooking time:* | 6 *mins* |
| Cooking apples, peeled, cored and sliced | 8 oz | 225g | ½ lb |
| Water | 1 tbsp | 15ml | 1 tbsp |
| Sugar | 2 tsp | 2 tsp | 2 tsp |
| Butter | ½ oz | 15g | 1 tbsp |
| Black pepper | | | |

*Method*
Place the apple slices in a suitable deep container, add the water and sprinkle over the sugar. Cover and cook for 6 minutes. Add the butter and pepper to taste. Mix well or liquidize before serving.

*Freezing:* Pour into a polythene or foil container, cool, cover, label and freeze.

## Chocolate Sauce

| | Imp. | Met. | Am. |
|---|---|---|---|
| Servings: 4 | | Cooking time: 2 mins | |
| Milk chocolate, broken into pieces | 4 oz | 100g | ¼ lb |
| Golden syrup | 3 tbsp | 3 tbsp | 3 tbsp |
| Butter | 1½ oz | 40g | 3 tbsp |
| Lemon juice | 2 tbsp | 30ml | 2 tbsp |

*Method*
Place all the ingredients into a suitable deep container. Cover and cook for 2 minutes. Beat the sauce vigorously with a wooden spoon until it is smooth and shiny. Serve with ice-cream or fruit such as bananas. If the sauce is allowed to cool it will heat up again in the microwave oven.

*Variation:* For a different flavour, orange juice and rind may be substituted for the lemon juice.

## Custard Sauce

| | Imp. | Met. | Am. |
|---|---|---|---|
| Servings: 4 | | Cooking time: 7 mins | |
| Custard powder | 2 tbsp | 2 tbsp | 2 tbsp |
| Sugar | 1–2 tbsp | 1–2 tbsp | 1–2 tbsp |
| Milk | 1 pt | 550ml | 2½ cups |

*Method*
Mix the custard powder and sugar with a little of the cold milk in a suitable deep bowl or jug. Stir in the remaining milk. Cook for about 7 minutes, stirring every 2 minutes, or until the custard is thick and creamy.

*Variations:* Flavourings may be added to the sauce such as vanilla, almond, nutmeg, mixed spice.

## Jam Sauce

| | *Imp.* | *Met.* | *Am.* |
|---|---|---|---|
| *Servings:* 4 | | *Cooking time:* 3–4 mins | |
| Water | ¼ pt | 150ml | ⅔ cup |
| Jam | 4 tbsp | 4 tbsp | 4 tbsp |
| Arrowroot | 2 tsp | 2 tsp | 2 tsp |

*Method*
Place the water and jam in a suitable deep container. Cover and cook for 2 minutes. Stir well. Mix the arrowroot with a little cold water to form a smooth paste. Stir this into the sauce and heat for a further 1–2 minutes until it thickens and becomes clear. Serve hot with sponge pudding or cold with ice cream.

## Caramel Sauce

| | *Imp.* | *Met.* | *Am.* |
|---|---|---|---|
| *Servings:* 4 | | *Cooking time:* 2 mins | |
| Caramel chocolate | 4 oz | 100g | ¼ lb |
| Butter | 1 oz | 25g | 2 tbsp |
| Milk | 2 tbsp | 30ml | 2 tbsp |

*Method*
Place all ingredients into a suitable deep container. Cover and cook for 2 minutes. Stir the sauce well before serving with ice cream.

## Butterscotch Sauce

*Servings:* 4                                      *Cooking time: 2 mins*

|              | Imp.    | Met.   | Am.    |
|--------------|---------|--------|--------|
| Butter       | 1 oz    | 25g    | 2 tbsp |
| Brown sugar  | 1 oz    | 25g    | 2 tbsp |
| Golden syrup | 1 tbsp  | 1 tbsp | 1 tbsp |
| Lemon juice  | ½ tsp   | 2·5ml  | ½ tsp  |

*Method*
Place all the ingredients into a suitable deep container. Cover and cook for 2 minutes. Stir the sauce well. Serve with ice cream.

# 14

# MEAT

With a microwave oven it is possible to serve a joint of meat within 1¼ hours of removal from the freezer. Joints, steaks, chops and casserole-type dishes can all be cooked in the microwave oven. Minced meat cooks well too since the meat fibres have already been partially broken up. It is worth remembering though that microwaves do not tenderize meat, so special care must be taken with the tougher cuts (see tips below).

Microwave cooking is a very clean method of cooking meat and perfect results can be obtained every time if a few basic rules are followed. Here are some guidelines.

*Tips for cooking meat*

Cooking times will vary greatly, according to the type, size and shape of the meat and its starting temperature. Manufacturer's instructions should be followed carefully. Ideally a joint should be of good quality and compact, about 5 in/ 125mm diameter. If it is boned and rolled then it should be securely tied with string. Cut off all but a small amount of surface fat. The following table may be used as a guide to cooking times:

|  |  | Minutes per 1 lb/450g |
| --- | --- | --- |
| Beef (a boneless joint will take | rare | 5–7 |
| less time than one with a | medium | $6\frac{1}{2}$–$8\frac{1}{2}$ |
| bone) | well done | $7\frac{1}{2}$–10 |
| Lamb (leg, shoulder) |  | 8–9 |
| Pork |  | 10–13 |
| Veal |  | 9–11 |

Covering meat during roasting prevents much splattering of fats and juices. Roasting bags therefore can be very useful. When using roasting bags, tie the opening with string and pierce the bag to allow steam to escape.

It is a good idea not to season with salt until *after* cooking since it absorbs moisture and causes the surface to dry out and toughen. Other seasonings may be used before cooking if liked (pepper, herbs, mustard, etc.).

Some manufacturers recommend the use of foil to protect small areas of a joint from overcooking. Your instruction book will state whether this is possible. Follow the instructions carefully and do not allow the foil to touch any part of the oven interior.

There will be some natural browning of a joint cooked in the microwave oven, but you may like to brown it quickly under a hot grill to crispen the surface after cooking. Joints will of course brown more if left uncovered during cooking, but there will be some loss of moisture and the oven walls will become heavily splashed. Small pieces of meat, such as chops, can be browned quickly in a frying pan before or after microwave cooking. In fact the flavour of a casserole is greatly improved if the meat is browned in a little fat before it is cooked in the microwave oven. Alternatively your oven may have a browning element, or hot air convection (please see pages 16 and 17) or a browning dish. A browning dish is pre-heated in the microwave oven until it is very hot. The meat is placed on the dish and the dish and meat are then put into the oven and the microwave energy switched on for the required time. During microwave cooking the meat should be turned over so that the other side is browned. Check with your instruction book for the correct use of these dishes. Joints of even shape will cook more evenly than, say a shoulder of lamb. For this reason it is a good idea to bone and roll odd-shaped joints.

A joint should be *turned over* half way through cooking. If your oven does not incorporate a turntable YOU WILL NEED TO TURN THE JOINT FREQUENTLY during microwave cooking to avoid overcooking in some areas.

Place a joint to be roasted on an upturned saucer (in a roasting bag or covered with cling film) in a large suitable container, so that it does not sit in its juices. Make sure of retaining every bit of flavour and goodness though by using the meat juices to make a sauce or gravy.

Microwave-cooked joints should be covered with foil and allowed to stand for 15–30 minutes before carving. The thick meat tissues retain the absorbed energy longer than other foods and the joint will continue cooking after it is removed from the microwave oven (rather like a boiled egg when it has been removed from a pan of boiling water). The absorbed heat is conducted to the centre of the joint. For this reason care should be taken not to overcook the meat since it will toughen.

Pork joints should always be very well cooked. If you enjoy crackling, simply cut the skin off the pork joint after cooking and crisp under a hot grill.

Do not use a meat thermometer in the microwave oven, unless it has been specifically designed for the purpose. It can however be placed in the thickest part of the meat once it has come out of the oven. Leave it in during the standing period.

Tender cuts of meat will cook more successfully than those tougher cuts which normally need long, slow cooking to soften the connective tissue. I have included two recipes using stewing meat in this section, and found the results most acceptable. If your oven has an automatic defrost setting, then this may be used to cook casseroles with tougher meat. It will still take less time than normal and the meat will be given a chance to soften. Tenderizing meat is a simpler matter if your oven has a variable control output (see page 18). Manufacturer's instructions will guide you on their best use. Soaking the cut meat in a marinade, such as tomato purée, cooking oil and lemon juice, will help tenderize the meat a little.

It is preferable to undercook meat in order to avoid it drying out. It can always be put back into the microwave oven for a few seconds or minutes extra.

*Thawing meat*
Thaw meat completely before microwave cooking if best results are to be obtained. Only small quantities may be thawed and cooked simultaneously. On average, thaw meat for about 2 minutes per 1 lb/450g, turning the piece over half way. After thawing, allow the meat to stand for 15–20 minutes before cooking.
  Meat is best thawed by subjecting it to short bursts of microwave energy with rests between (simple if your oven has an automatic defrost button).
  Cooked meat and cooked meat dishes may be thawed and reheated in the microwave oven.


## Beef with Horseradish

*Servings:* 4  *Cooking time: 24 mins*

| | Imp. | Met. | Am. |
|---|---|---|---|
| Beef joint, such as top rump | 2½ lb | 1kg | 2½ lb |
| Cornflour (cornstarch) | 1 tbsp | 1 tbsp | 1 tbsp |
| Horseradish sauce | 2 tbsp | 2 tbsp | 2 tbsp |
| Water | ¼ pt | 150ml | ⅔ cup |
| Salt and black pepper | | | |

*Method*

Put the beef joint into a roasting bag (tie the opening with string and pierce the bag). Place it on an upturned saucer in a suitable large container. Cook for 20 minutes for medium-cooked beef (see chart on page 66 for rare or well-cooked beef). Allow to stand for 20–30 minutes. Take the joint out of the roasting bag and place on a carving dish. In a suitable container mix the cornflour with a little cold water to form a smooth paste. Add the juices from the beef and stir well. Add the remaining ingredients and cook for 4 minutes, stirring twice. Serve the sauce separately.

*Freezing:* Slices of beef may be placed in a freezer-to-microwave or polythene container, sauce poured over, cooled, covered, labelled and frozen.

## Beef Casserole

| *Servings:* 4 | Imp. | *Cooking time:* 30 mins Met. | Am. |
|---|---|---|---|
| Cooking oil | 2 tbsp | 30ml | 2 tbsp |
| Stewing steak, cut into cubes | 1½ lb | 700g | 1½ lb |
| Large onion, chopped | 1 | 1 | 1 |
| Celery stalks (sticks), chopped | 4 | 4 | 4 |
| Potato, cut into small cubes | 1 | 1 | 1 |
| Courgette (squash), sliced | 1 | 1 | 1 |
| Flour | 1 oz | 25g | ¼ cup |
| English mustard, made | 1 tsp | 1 tsp | 1 tsp |
| Beef stock (bouillon) | 1 pt | 500ml | 2½ cups |
| Bouquet garni | 1 | 1 | 1 |
| Salt and pepper | | | |

*Method*

Heat the cooking oil in a large frying pan and brown the beef quickly on all sides. Stir in the onion, celery, potato and courgette and cook for a further 2 minutes. Stir in the flour then add the mustard, stock, bouquet garni and seasoning to taste. Bring to the boil and transfer to a large suitable casserole. Cover and cook for 30 minutes, stirring twice. Allow to stand for 15 minutes before removing bouquet garni and serving.

*Freezing:* Pour into a freezer-to-microwave or polythene container, cool, cover, label and freeze.

## Burgundy Beef and Peppers

| *Servings:* 4 | | *Cooking time:* 14 *mins* | |
|---|---|---|---|
| | *Imp.* | *Met.* | *Am.* |
| **Cooking oil** | 2 tbsp | 30ml | 2 tbsp |
| **Large onion, chopped** | 1 | 1 | 1 |
| **Sirloin steak, cut into** | | | |
| **cubes** | 1¾ lb | 800g | 1¾ lb |
| **Red wine** | ¾ pt | 400ml | 2 cups |
| **Chilli powder** | 1 tsp | 1 tsp | 1 tsp |
| **Bouquet garni** | 1 | 1 | 1 |
| **Tomato purée (paste)** | 2 tbsp | 2 tbsp | 2 tbsp |
| **Salt and pepper** | | | |
| **Large carrot, cut into** | | | |
| **strips** | 1 | 1 | 1 |
| **Green pepper, deseeded** | | | |
| **and sliced thinly** | 1–2 | 1–2 | 1–2 |

*Method*
Place the cooking oil and onion in a suitable container, cover and cook for 3 minutes. Stir in the steak and cook, covered, for 4 minutes, stirring twice. Add the remaining ingredients, cover and cook for 7 minutes, stirring once. Allow to stand covered for 10–15 minutes before removing bouquet garni, adjusting seasoning if necessary, and serving. Delicious with green salad.

*Freezing:* Pour into a freezer-to-microwave or polythene container, cool, cover, label and freeze.

# All Seasons Pie

*Servings:* 4                                              *Cooking time:* 25 *mins*

|  | Imp. | Met. | Am. |
|---|---|---|---|
| Cooking oil | 1 tbsp | 15ml | 1 tbsp |
| Onions, chopped | 2 | 2 | 2 |
| Minced (ground) beef | 1 lb | 450g | 1 lb |
| Beef stock cube (bouillon) crumbled | 1 | 1 | 1 |
| Dried mixed peppers | 1 tbsp | 1 tbsp | 1 tbsp |
| Salt and pepper |  |  |  |
| Mixed herbs | 1 tsp | 1 tsp | 1 tsp |
| Tomato purée (paste) | 1 tbsp | 1 tbsp | 1 tbsp |
| Flour | 2 tsp | 2 tsp | 2 tsp |
| Water | 3 tbsp | 45ml | 3 tbsp |
| Potatoes, thinly sliced | 1½ lb | 700g | 1½ lb |

*Method*

Place the cooking oil and onions in a large suitable container, cover and cook for 3 minutes. Add the minced beef, stock cube, peppers, seasoning, and tomato purée. Mix the flour with the water to form a smooth paste and add this to the mince mixture. Stir well, cover and cook for 7 minutes, stirring twice. Layer the potato slices, seasoning each layer with salt and pepper, and dot the butter over the top. Cover and cook for 15 minutes. Allow to stand for 15 minutes before serving. This dish looks very attractive if placed under a hot grill for a few minutes to brown and crisp the surface.

*Freezing:* Cool, cover, label and freeze.

*Variation:* This recipe may also be prepared with minced lamb.

# Beefburgers in Spicy Sauce

*Servings:* 4                                              *Cooking time:* 15 *mins*

|  | Imp. | Met. | Am. |
|---|---|---|---|
| Minced (ground) beef | 1 lb | 450g | 1 lb |
| Medium onion, chopped | 1 | 1 | 1 |
| Mixed herbs | 1 tsp | 1 tsp | 1 tsp |

## Beefburgers in Spicy Sauce—contd.

| | | | |
|---|---|---|---|
| Tabasco sauce | few drops | few drops | few d'ps |
| Tomato purée (paste) | 1 tbsp | 1 tbsp | 1 tbsp |
| Egg, beaten | 1 | 1 | 1 |
| Seasoned flour | | | |
| Cooking oil | 2 tbsp | 30ml | 2 tbsp |
| **Sauce:** | | | |
| Horseradish sauce | 1 tbsp | 1 tbsp | 1 tbsp |
| Tabasco sauce | few drops | few drops | few d'ps |
| Worcestershire sauce | 1 tbsp | 15ml | 1 tbsp |
| Salt and pepper | | | |
| Tomato purée (paste) | 1 tbsp | 1 tbsp | 1 tbsp |
| Beef stock cube (bouillon), crumbled | 1 | 1 | 1 |
| Water | ¼ pt | 150ml | ⅔ cup |
| Cornflour (cornstarch) | 2 tsp | 2 tsp | 2 tsp |

*Method*

Mix together the beef, onions, herbs, Tabasco sauce and tomato purée and shape into four beefburgers. Coat with beaten egg then seasoned flour. Heat the cooking oil in a large frying pan and brown the beefburgers quickly on both sides. Arrange in a suitable shallow casserole. Cook, uncovered for 5 minutes. Mix together the ingredients for the sauce and pour round the beefburgers. Cover and cook for 10 minutes.

*Freezing:* Arrange the beefburgers in a freezer-to-microwave or polythene container, pour the sauce round, cool, cover, label and freeze.

## Minted Lamb

*Servings:* 6          *Cooking time:* 31 *mins*

| | Imp. | Met. | Am. |
|---|---|---|---|
| Leg of Lamb | 3½ lb | 1·6kg | 3½ lb |
| Garlic cloves, cut into slithers | 1–2 | 1–2 | 1–2 |
| Mint, chopped finely | 2 tbsp | 2 tbsp | 2 tbsp |
| Vinegar | 2 tsp | 10ml | 2 tsp |
| Sugar | 1 tsp | 1 tsp | 1 tsp |
| Salt and black pepper | | | |

*Method*
Cut small slits in the surface of the lamb and insert the garlic slithers. Put the joint into a roasting bag (tie the opening with string and pierce the bag). Place the lamb on an upturned saucer in a large suitable container. Cook for 30 minutes, turning the joint over once during cooking. Allow to stand for 20–30 minutes. Pour the juices from the lamb into a suitable small container and mix in the chopped mint, vinegar and sugar. Season well with salt and black pepper. Cook for 1 minute or until the sauce boils. Stir well and pour over the joint before carving. If liked, a thicker consistency may be obtained by adding 1 tsp. cornflour (cornstarch) mixed with a little cold water.

*Freezing:* Wrap leftover slices of lamb in foil to freeze, or arrange slices in a freezer-to-microwave or polythene container and pour some sauce over. Cool, cover, label and freeze.
*Variation:* Substitute other herbs for the mint.

## Crown Roast with Fruit Stuffing

*Servings:* 6

*Cooking time:* 40 *mins*

| | Imp. | Met. | Am. |
|---|---|---|---|
| Best end neck lamb, 2 pieces about 12 chops | 3 lb | 1·4kg | 3 lb |
| Salt and pepper | | | |
| Small onion, chopped finely | 1 | 1 | 1 |
| Small carrot, grated | 1 | 1 | 1 |
| Apple, peeled, cored and grated | 1 | 1 | 1 |
| Juice and rind of orange | 1 | 1 | 1 |
| Sultanas | 1 oz | 25g | 2 tbsp |
| Breadcrumbs | 4 oz | 100g | 2 cups |
| Cider or water | 2 tbsp | 30ml | 2 tbsp |

*Method*
Ask your butcher to chop through the thick ends of the chops so that the pieces will curve. Trim the top 1 inch (25mm) of each bone, cutting off meat and fat. Chop these trimmings

finely (not including too much fat). Using a trussing needle and string, truss the two pieces to form a crown as in fig. 7 (skin side in). Season with salt and pepper. In a bowl, mix together the remaining ingredients with the chopped lamb

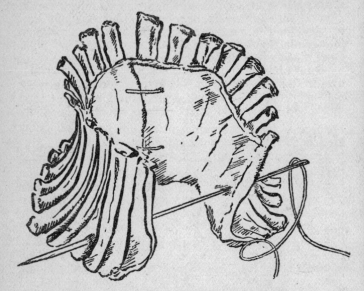

**Fig. 7. Crown Roast With Fruit Stuffing.**
(Joining the two pieces of lamb with string and a trussing needle.)

trimmings and seasoning to taste. Use this mixture to stuff the lamb crown, pressing in firmly. Place the joint in a suitable large container. Cook uncovered for about 40 minutes, depending on the thickness of the chops. Allow to stand for 20–30 minutes before serving. Place a paper ruffle on the tip of each chop (or, with the fruit stuffing, a grape on the tip of each chop looks good too).

# Apricot Lamb Chops

| | Imp. | Met. | Am. |
|---|---|---|---|
| *Servings:* 4 | | *Cooking time:* 15 *mins* | |
| Lamb, loin chops | 4 | 4 | 4 |
| Tomatoes, skinned and chopped | 2 | 2 | 2 |
| Onion, chopped finely | 1 | 1 | 1 |
| Can apricots, drained and chopped | 7½ oz | 213g | small |
| Tomato purée (paste) | 2 tbsp | 2 tbsp | 2 tbsp |
| Salt and black pepper | | | |
| Chopped parsley | 1 tbsp | 1 tbsp | 1 tbsp |

*Method*
Place the lamb chops in a large suitable shallow container. In a bowl mix together the tomatoes, onion, apricots, tomato purée and seasoning. Spread the mixture over each chop. Cook uncovered for 15 minutes. Allow to stand for 15 minutes before serving. Reheat if necessary. Garnish with the chopped parsley.

# Lamb and Courgette Casserole

| | Imp. | Met. | Am. |
|---|---|---|---|
| *Servings:* 4 | | *Cooking time:* 35 *mins* | |
| Cooking oil | 2 tbsp | 30ml | 2 tbsp |
| Lamb, lean, cut into cubes | 1½ lb | 700g | 1½ lb |
| Seasoned flour | 2 tsp | 2 tsp | 2 tsp |
| Onions, chopped | 8 oz | 225g | ½ lb |
| Can tomatoes, including juice | 14 oz | 397g | medium |
| Mint jelly | 3 tbsp | 3 tbsp | 3 tbsp |
| Bay leaf | 1 | 1 | 1 |
| Salt and black pepper | | | |
| Courgettes (squash), sliced | 8 oz | 225g | ½ lb |

*Method*
Heat the cooking oil in a large frying pan. Coat the lamb in seasoned flour and brown quickly in the hot oil. Stir in the

onions and cook for a further minute. Stir in the tomatoes, mint jelly, bay leaf and seasoning. Bring to the boil and transfer to a suitable large casserole. Cover and cook in the microwave oven for 30 minutes, stirring twice. Add the courgettes and mix well. Cover and cook for a further 5 minutes. The courgettes should still have a slight bite. Allow to stand for 15 minutes before removing bay leaf and serving.

*Freezing:* Better frozen without the courgettes since they need to be slightly crunchy on serving. Pour into a freezer-to-microwave or polythene container, cool, cover, label and freeze.

## Apricot Stuffed Pork

| *Servings:* 4–6 | | *Cooking time:* 38 *mins* | |
|---|---|---|---|
| | *Imp.* | *Met.* | *Am.* |
| Small onion, chopped | 1 | 1 | 1 |
| Celery stick (stalk), chopped | 1 | 1 | 1 |
| Butter | 1½ oz | 40g | 3 tbsp |
| Breadcrumbs | 2 oz | 50g | 1 cup |
| Parsley, chopped | 2 tbsp | 2 tbsp | 2 tbsp |
| Salt and pepper | | | |
| Can apricot halves | 10 oz | 284g | medium |
| Pork joint, such as leg fillet, boned and rind removed | 3 lb | 1½kg | 3 lb |

*Method*

Place the onion, celery and butter in a suitable deep container, cover and cook for 3 minutes, stirring once. Add the breadcrumbs, parsley and seasoning and mix well. Chop 6 apricot halves and add these along with 2 tbsp/30ml of the apricot syrup. Mix well and use to stuff the pork joint. Tie the joint securely with string and put it into a roasting bag (tie the opening with string and pierce the bag to allow steam to escape). Place on an upturned saucer in a suitable, large container. Cook for 35 minutes. Allow the joint to stand for 20–30 minutes then remove from the roasting bag (make sure it is well cooked throughout). If liked, brown the fat side of the pork under a hot grill. Slice the meat and serve garnished with the remaining apricot halves. Reheat for a few minutes if necessary.

*Variation:* Substitute a can of prunes for the apricots.

## Pork and Bean Casserole

| Servings: 4 | | Cooking time: 35 mins | |
|---|---|---|---|
| | Imp. | Met. | Am. |
| Butter | 1 oz | 25g | 2 tbsp |
| Cooking oil | 1 tbsp | 15ml | 1 tbsp |
| Lean pork, cut into cubes | 1½ lb | 700g | 1½ lb |
| Onions, chopped finely | 8 oz | 225g | ½ lb |
| Can tomatoes, roughly chopped, including juice | 14 oz | 397g | medium |
| Chicken or onion stock cube | 1 | 1 | 1 |
| Tomato purée (paste) | 1 tbsp | 1 tbsp | 1 tbsp |
| Mixed herbs | 1 tsp | 1 tsp | 1 tsp |
| Salt and pepper | | | |
| Can red kidney beans, drained | 15¼ oz | 432g | medium |

*Method*
Heat the butter and cooking oil in a large frying pan and brown the pork on all sides. Add the onions and cook for a further 2 minutes. Transfer to a suitable deep casserole then stir in the tomatoes, crumbled stock cube, tomato purée, herbs and seasoning. Cover and cook for 30 minutes, stirring twice. Stir in the drained beans, cover and cook for a further 5 minutes. Allow to stand for 15 minutes before serving.

*Freezing:* Pour into a freezer-to-microwave or polythene container, cool, cover, label and freeze.

## Honey Spare-Ribs

*Servings:* 4                                   *Cooking time:* 25 mins

|  | Imp. | Met. | Am. |
|---|---|---|---|
| Clear honey | 3 tbsp | 3 tbsp | 3 tbsp |
| White wine | 4 tbsp | 60ml | 4 tbsp |
| Wine vinegar | 2 tbsp | 30ml | 2 tbsp |
| Chutney (such as tomato and apple) | 2 tbsp | 2 tbsp | 2 tbsp |
| Dried mixed peppers | 2 tbsp | 2 tbsp | 2 tbsp |
| French mustard | 2 tsp | 2 tsp | 2 tsp |
| Cornflour (cornstarch) | 1 tbsp | 1 tbsp | 1 tbsp |
| Salt and pepper | | | |
| Pork spare ribs | 2 lb | 900g | 2 lb |

*Method*

In a suitable large, shallow casserole, mix together the honey, wine, wine vinegar, chutney, peppers, mustard, cornflour and seasoning. Heat in the microwave oven for 1 minute to soften then stir the mixture well. Add the spare ribs and coat well with the sauce. Marinate for at least 1 hour, stirring occasionally. Cover and cook for 15 minutes, basting twice during cooking. Remove cover, baste again and cook for a further 10 minutes. Allow to stand for 15 minutes before serving with hot plain rice.

## Chinese Pork and Vegetables

*Servings:* 4                                   *Cooking time:* 26 mins

|  | Imp. | Met. | Am. |
|---|---|---|---|
| Cooking oil | 2 tbsp | 30ml | 2 tbsp |
| Onions, sliced thinly | 8 oz | 225g | ½ lb |
| Carrots, sliced thinly | 4 oz | 100g | ¼ lb |
| Red pepper, deseeded and sliced thinly | 1 | 1 | 1 |
| Pork fillet, cut into thin strips | 1 lb | 450g | 1 lb |
| Cabbage, shredded | 8 oz | 225g | ½ lb |
| Sugar | 2 tsp | 2 tsp | 2 tsp |
| Cornflour (cornstarch) | 1 tbsp | 1 tbsp | 1 tbsp |

| | Imp. | Met. | Am. |
|---|---|---|---|
| Chicken stock | ¼ pt | 150ml | ⅔ cup |
| Soy sauce | 2 tbsp | 30ml | 2 tbsp |
| Large flat mushroom, sliced | 1 | 1 | 1 |
| Salt and pepper | | | |

*Method*

Place the cooking oil, onions, carrots and red pepper into a suitable large casserole. Cover and cook for 3 minutes. Stir in the pork strips, cover and cook for 15 minutes, stirring 3 or 4 times to separate the meat. Stir in the remaining ingredients, cover and cook for 8 minutes. Allow to stand for 15 minutes before serving. Good with noodles.

*Freezing:* This dish may be frozen but the vegetables will not have the characteristic crispness after thawing and reheating. Pour into a freezer-to-microwave or polythene container, cool, cover, label and freeze.

## Apple Stuffed Pork Chops

*Servings:* 4                     *Cooking time:* 15 *mins*

| | Imp. | Met. | Am. |
|---|---|---|---|
| Pork chops, large | 4 | 4 | 4 |
| Breadcrumbs | 6 tbsp | 6 tbsp | 6 tbsp |
| Eating apples, skinned, cored and chopped finely or grated | 2 | 2 | 2 |
| Onion, chopped finely, or grated | 1 | 1 | 1 |
| Sultanas | 1 tbsp | 1 tbsp | 1 tbsp |
| Mixed herbs | ½ tsp | ½ tsp | ½ tsp |
| Salt and black pepper | | | |
| Milk to mix | | | |

*Method*

Remove the rind from the chops then cut a deep slit in the fat edge of each to form a pocket for the stuffing.

Mix together the breadcrumbs, apples, onion, sultanas, herbs and seasoning. Moisten with a little milk. Fill the chops with the mixture and secure each with a wooden cocktail stick if necessary. Cook uncovered for 15 minutes. Allow to stand for 15 minutes before serving, reheating if necessary.

*Variations:* Try your own favourite stuffing to replace the apple stuffing.

## Autumn Bacon Casserole

| *Servings:* 4 | *Cooking time:* 35 mins + boiling | | |
|---|---|---|---|
| | *Imp.* | *Met.* | *Am.* |
| Smoked bacon joint, such as collar, cut into cubes | 1½ lb | 700g | 1½ lb |
| Butter | 1 oz | 25g | 2 tbsp |
| Flour | 2 tbsp | 2 tbsp | 2 tbsp |
| Leeks, chopped | 8 oz | 225g | ½ lb |
| Large carrot, cut into thin strips | 1 | 1 | 1 |
| Can tomatoes, including juice | 14 oz | 397g | medium |
| Silverskin onions, drained | 2 tbsp | 2 tbsp | 2 tbsp |
| Frozen sweetcorn kernels | 4 tbsp | 4 tbsp | 4 tbsp |
| Water | ½ pt | 300ml | 1¼ cups |
| Black pepper | | | |

*Method*
Place the bacon cubes in a large saucepan and cover well with cold water. Bring slowly to the boil on the hob then discard the water. Dry the bacon cubes with kitchen paper. Place the bacon and butter in a suitable casserole, cover and cook for 5 minutes, stirring once. Stir in the flour then add the remaining ingredients. Cover and cook for 30 minutes, stirring twice. Allow to stand for 15 minutes before serving. Delicious with baked potatoes.

*Freezing:* Pour into freezer-to-microwave or polythene container, cool, cover, label and freeze.

## Bacon with Pineapple

| *Servings:* 6–8 | | *Cooking time:* 32 mins | |
|---|---|---|---|
| | Imp. | Met. | Am. |
| Smoked bacon joint | 3 lb | 1·4kg | 3 lb |
| Can pineapple rings | 1 lb 13 oz | 822g | large |
| Black pepper | | | |
| Cornflour (cornstarch) | 1 tbsp | 1 tbsp | 1 tbsp |
| Green pepper, deseeded | | | |
| and chopped finely | 2 tbsp | 2 tbsp | 2 tbsp |

*Method*

Place the bacon joint in a large saucepan and cover with cold water. Bring to the boil and discard the water. Dry the joint with kitchen paper and place in a suitable deep container. Pour round the juice from the pineapple and season with black pepper. Cover and cook for 30 minutes, turning the joint over after 15 minutes. Place the bacon on a carving dish and allow to stand for about 15 minutes. Meanwhile mix the cornflour with a little cold water to form a smooth paste. Stir this into the pineapple juice then add the green pepper. Cook for 2 minutes or until the sauce thickens. Carve the bacon and arrange on a serving dish. Arrange the pineapple rings on top and then pour over the sauce. Reheat for 2–3 minutes if necessary.

*Freezing:* Arrange bacon slices in a freezer-to-microwave or polythene container, pour some sauce over, cool, cover, label and freeze. Do not freeze the pineapple rings.

*Variation:* A can of apricots may replace the pineapple.

## Savoury Veal Casserole

| *Servings:* 4 | | *Cooking time:* 25 mins + frying | |
|---|---|---|---|
| | Imp. | Met. | Am. |
| Cooking oil | 2 tbsp | 30ml | 2 tbsp |
| Stewing veal, cut into | | | |
| small pieces | 1¾ lb | 800g | 1¾ lb |
| Onion, chopped | 1 | 1 | 1 |
| Can tomatoes, | | | |
| including juice | 14 oz | 397g | medium |

## Savoury Veal Casserole—contd.

| | | | |
|---|---|---|---|
| Tomato purée (paste) | 1 tbsp | 1 tbsp | 1 tbsp |
| Beef stock (bouillon) | ¼ pt | 150ml | ⅔ cup |
| Bay leaf | 1 | 1 | 1 |
| Ground ginger | ½ tsp | ½ tsp | ½ tsp |
| Salt and black pepper | | | |
| Mushrooms, quartered | 4 oz | 100g | ¼ lb |
| Flour | 2 tbsp | 2 tbsp | 2 tbsp |

*Method*

Heat the cooking oil in a large frying pan and brown the veal quickly. Stir in the onion, tomatoes, tomato purée, beef stock, bay leaf, ginger and seasoning. Bring to the boil and transfer to a suitable deep casserole. Cover and cook for 20 minutes. Stir in the mushrooms. Mix the flour with a little cold water to form a smooth paste. Stir into the casserole. Cover and cook for a further 5 minutes. Allow to stand for 15 minutes before serving.

*Freezing:* Pour into a freezer-to-microwave or polythene container, cool, cover, label and freeze.

## Veal with Wine and Almonds

*Servings:* 4    *Cooking time:* 22 *mins*

| | Imp. | Met. | Am. |
|---|---|---|---|
| Butter | 1 oz | 25g | 2 tbsp |
| Onion, chopped finely | 4 tbsp | 4 tbsp | 4 tbsp |
| White wine | ½ pt | 300ml | 1¼ cups |
| Veal escalopes | 4 | 4 | 4 |
| Salt and pepper | | | |
| Double (thick) cream | 4 tbsp | 4 tbsp | 4 tbsp |
| Flaked almonds | 1 tbsp | 1 tbsp | 1 tbsp |
| Parsley, chopped | 1 tbsp | 1 tbsp | 1 tbsp |

*Method*

Place the butter and onion into a suitable casserole, cover and cook for 3 minutes. Stir in the wine and add the veal. Season to taste with salt and pepper. Cover and cook for 15 minutes, stirring twice. Allow to stand for 15 minutes. Before serving, reheat (about 4 minutes) then stir in the cream and sprinkle over the almonds and parsley. Do not reheat after adding the cream.

*Freezing:* Do not add the cream, almonds or parsley. Arrange the veal in a freezer-to-microwave or polythene container, cool, cover, label and freeze.

## Orange Liver and Bacon

| *Servings:* 4 | | *Cooking time:* 13 *mins* | |
|---|---|---|---|
| | *Imp.* | *Met.* | *Am.* |
| **Large onion, chopped** | **1** | **1** | **1** |
| **Bacon, unsmoked, cut into small pieces** | **4 oz** | **100g** | **¼ lb** |
| **Cooking oil** | **2 tbsp** | **30ml** | **2 tbsp** |
| **Lamb's liver, sliced thinly** | **1 lb** | **450g** | **1 lb** |
| **Flour** | **1 oz** | **25g** | **¼ cup** |
| **Salt and pepper** | | | |
| **Rind and juice of oranges** | **2** | **2** | **2** |
| **Beef stock (bouillon) hot** | **¼ pt** | **150ml** | **⅔ cup** |
| **Chopped parsley** | **2 tbsp** | **2 tbsp** | **2 tbsp** |

*Method*
Place the onion, bacon and cooking oil in a suitable large container, cover and cook for 3 minutes. Coat the liver pieces with the flour and stir into the onion mixture. Season to taste with salt and pepper. Mix together the orange rind and juice and the stock and pour over the liver. Cover and cook for 10 minutes, stirring once. Allow to stand for 10–15 minutes then sprinkle over the chopped parsley to serve.

## Kidneys in Mushroom Sauce

| *Servings:* 4 | | *Cooking time:* 12 *mins* | |
|---|---|---|---|
| | *Imp.* | *Met.* | *Am.* |
| **Butter** | **1 oz** | **25g** | **2 tbsp** |
| **Onion, chopped** | **1** | **1** | **1** |
| **Lambs' kidneys, skinned, cored and sliced** | **8** | **8** | **8** |
| **Mushrooms, quartered** | **8 oz** | **225g** | **½ lb** |

## Kidneys in Mushroom Sauce—contd.

| | | | |
|---|---|---|---|
| Cornflour (cornstarch) | 4 tbsp | 4 tbsp | 4 tbsp |
| Beef stock (bouillon) | ½ pt | 300ml | 1¼ cups |
| Tomato purée (paste) | 1 tbsp | 1 tbsp | 1 tbsp |
| Salt and pepper | | | |
| Parsley, chopped | 3 tbsp | 3 tbsp | 3 tbsp |

*Method*
Place the butter and onion in a suitable container. Cover and cook for 2 minutes. Add the kidneys and cook for 5 minutes, stirring once. Stir in the mushrooms, cornflour, stock, tomato purée and seasoning to taste. Cover and cook for 5 minutes, stirring once, until the mixture is thick. Allow to stand for 5 minutes then stir in the parsley. Serve with hot rice or duchesse potatoes.

*Freezing:* Omit parsley. Pour into freezer-to-microwave or polythene container, cool, cover, label and freeze.

*Variation:* Replace the beef stock with a rich red wine for Kidneys in Red Wine.

# 15

# Poultry

Poultry cooked in a microwave oven is both tender and moist. Whole birds or joints are prepared speedily and with little effort. Whether roasting or casseroling I guarantee that the result will be one of the most succulent you have ever tasted.

*Tips for cooking poultry*
The cooking time for a whole bird will depend on its type, size and age. A good guide is 6–8 minutes per 1 lb/450g. Use the recipes that follow for guidance on cooking times for joints and when adapting your own recipes for microwave cooking.

Take care not to overcook poultry or the result will be tough and dry. On the other hand, make sure it is well cooked. A good rule is to cook for the minimum time suggested then allow the bird or joints to stand covered. If necessary it can be put back into the microwave oven for a few minutes more.

In general, poultry should be covered during cooking. Roasting bags are ideal for microwave cooking poultry. A whole bird may be placed in a roasting bag (tie the opening with string and pierce the bag to allow steam to escape), or simply cover with a piece of kitchen paper or greaseproof paper to prevent splattering and to aid the basting process.
　　Turn a whole bird over half-way through cooking. Unless your oven has a turntable the poultry should be moved about or rotated in the oven several times to ensure even cooking.

Foil can be used to shield the thin parts of the legs if recommended by the oven manufacturer. Do not allow the foil to touch any part of the oven interior.

When roasting, poultry should be placed on an upturned saucer in a large container so that it is raised above its juices. Use these juices though for making gravy.

Unless your oven has a browning element, a browning dish or hot air convection (see pages 16 and 17), you may like to put the cooked bird under a hot grill to crispen the skin, or put it in a pre-heated hot oven for 10-15 minutes. If not, a good 'disguising' glaze is achieved if the bird is brushed with melted butter before cooking. A sprinkling of paprika over the breast side of a cooked chicken is also attractive.

After cooking cover the poultry with foil and allow it to stand for 15–20 minutes so that the heat penetrates all parts of the bird equally.

Meat thermometers should not be placed in the microwave oven (unless specifically designed for this use). Place the thermometer deep in the thigh of the cooked bird while it is standing after cooking.

Season with salt *after* cooking since it tends to dry out and toughen the surface of the bird.

Poultry joints are best skinned if they are to be microwave cooked (particularly if they are to be cooked in a sauce). This improves the appearance of the finished dish for the skins will not crisp in the microwave oven.

Browning joints in the frying pan before microwave cooking improves the flavour.

Boiling fowl should only be used for stock and soup-making since they will toughen in the microwave oven.

*Thawing poultry*
It is important to thaw all poultry thoroughly before cooking. After thawing allow the poultry to stand for 15–20 minutes (30 minutes for whole large birds) before cooking.
  Poultry is best subjected to short bursts of microwave energy with rests between. This avoids cooking the thinner parts accidentally and is a simple matter if your oven incorporates an automatic defrost button.
  Follow manufacturer's instructions for correct thawing times for poultry.

## Rich Chicken Tomato Casserole

*Servings:* 4          *Cooking time:* 25–35 *mins*

|  | Imp. | Met. | Am. |
| --- | --- | --- | --- |
| Cooking oil | 1 tbsp | 15ml | 1 tbsp |
| Butter | 1 oz | 25g | 2 tbsp |
| Chicken portions, skinned | 4 | 4 | 4 |
| Flour | 2 tbsp | 2 tbsp | 2 tbsp |
| Can tomatoes, including juice | 1 lb 12 oz | 794g | large |
| Chicken stock cube, crumbled | 1 | 1 | 1 |
| Bay leaves | 2 | 2 | 2 |
| Oregano | 1 tsp | 1 tsp | 1 tsp |
| Lemon juice | 1 tbsp | 15ml | 1 tbsp |
| Salt and black pepper |  |  |  |

*Method*
Heat the cooking oil and butter in a large frying pan and brown the chicken portions well on all sides. Transfer to a suitable large casserole. Add the flour to the remaining fat in the frying pan. Stir well and cook for about 1 minute. Stir in the remaining ingredients, bring to the boil and pour over the chicken. Cover and cook for 25–35 minutes, depending on the size of the chicken pieces. Remove bay leaves before serving.

*Freezing:* Place in a freezer-to-microwave or polythene container, cool, cover, label and freeze.

## Chicken with White Wine

*Servings:* 4          *Cooking time:* 36 *mins*

|  | Imp. | Met. | Am. |
| --- | --- | --- | --- |
| Chicken, whole | 3½ lb | 1·6kg | 3½ lb |
| Tarragon | ½–1 tsp | ½–1 tsp | ½–1 tsp |
| Salt and pepper |  |  |  |
| White wine, dry | ½ pt | 300ml | 1¼ cups |
| Bay leaves | 2 | 2 | 2 |
| Black peppercorns | 6 | 6 | 6 |
| Carrot, peeled and quartered | 1 | 1 | 1 |

## Chicken with White Wine—contd.

| | Imp. | Met. | Am. |
|---|---|---|---|
| **Onion, peeled and quartered** | 1 | 1 | 1 |
| **Chicken stock** | ½ pt | 300ml | 1¼ cups |
| **Cornflour (cornstarch)** | 2 tbsp | 2 tbsp | 2 tbsp |

*Method*
Place the chicken in a large suitable casserole and sprinkle over the tarragon and seasoning. Pour round the wine and add the bay leaves, peppercorns, carrot, onion and chicken stock. Cover and cook for 30 minutes. Allow to stand for about 20 minutes. Place the chicken on a serving dish. Strain the sauce. Return the strained liquid to the casserole. Mix the cornflour with a little cold water to form a smooth paste and stir into the sauce. Cook uncovered for 6 minutes, stirring 2 or 3 times. Adjust seasoning if necessary. Serve the sauce with the carved chicken.

*Freezing:* Place pieces of the chicken in a freezer-to-microwave or polythene container, pour some sauce over, cool, cover, label and freeze.

## Maryland Chicken

*Servings:* 4                         *Cooking time: 26½ mins*

| | Imp. | Met. | Am. |
|---|---|---|---|
| **Cooking oil** | 2 tbsp | 30ml | 2 tbsp |
| **Large onion, sliced finely** | 1 | 1 | 1 |
| **Celery stick (stalk), chopped** | 1 | 1 | 1 |
| **Chicken thighs, skinned** | 4 | 4 | 4 |
| **Salt and pepper** | | | |
| **Flour** | 2 tbsp | 2 tbsp | 2 tbsp |
| **Chicken stock, hot** | ¾ pt | 400ml | 2 cups |
| **Mustard, made up** | 1 tsp | 1 tsp | 1 tsp |
| **Mixed herbs** | 1 tsp | 1 tsp | 1 tsp |
| **Can sweetcorn, drained** | 7 oz | 198g | small |
| **Banana, sliced thickly** | 1 | 1 | 1 |
| **Bacon rashers (slices)** | 2 | 2 | 2 |

*Method*
Place the cooking oil, onion and celery in a suitable deep container, cover and cook for 4 minutes. Season the chicken pieces with salt and pepper and arrange these on top of the onion mixture. Mix the flour with a little cold water to form a smooth paste then stir in to the hot stock carefully. Add the mustard and herbs and pour over the chicken. Cover and cook for 15 minutes. Stir in the drained sweetcorn, cover and cook for 4 minutes. Arrange the banana slices on top of the chicken, cover and cook for 2 minutes. Allow to stand for 10–15 minutes before serving. Meanwhile cut the rind off the bacon and stretch the rasher carefully with the flat side of a knife. Cut each rasher in half and roll up into 4 curls. Place these on a plate and cook, uncovered for 1½ minutes. Use to garnish the chicken.

*Freezing:* Omit banana and bacon. Place in a freezer-to-microwave or polythene container, cool, cover, label and freeze.

## Chicken Oriental

*Servings:* 4                                   *Cooking time: 30 mins*

|  | Imp. | Met. | Am. |
|---|---|---|---|
| Butter | 1 oz | 25g | 2 tbsp |
| Onions, chopped | 8 oz | 225g | ½ lb |
| Tarragon | 1 tsp | 1 tsp | 1 tsp |
| Chilli powder | ¼ tsp | ¼ tsp | ¼ tsp |
| Coriander | ¼ tsp | ¼ tsp | ¼ tsp |
| Turmeric | ½ tsp | ½ tsp | ½ tsp |
| Chicken stock cube, crumbled | ½ | ½ | ½ |
| Pineapple juice, unsweetened | ½ pt | 300ml | 1¼ cups |
| Chicken breasts, bone left in, skinned and seasoned | 4 | 4 | 4 |
| Cornflour (cornstarch) | 1½ tbsp | 1½ tbsp | 1½ tbsp |

*Method*
Place the butter and onions into a suitable container, cover and cook for 3 minutes. Stir in the tarragon, chilli powder,

coriander, turmeric, stock cube and pineapple juice and mix together well. Add the chicken breasts and make sure they are coated well with the sauce. Cover and cook for 25 minutes (30 minutes if the chicken pieces are very large). Arrange the chicken pieces in a serving dish. Mix the cornflour with a little cold water to form a smooth paste and stir into the sauce. Cook for 2 minutes, stirring every ½ minute. Pour over the chicken and serve with rice and green salad.

## Turkey Special

| *Servings*: 4 | | *Cooking time:* 21–26 *mins* | |
|---|---|---|---|
| | *Imp.* | *Met.* | *Am.* |
| **Garlic clove, halved** | 1 | 1 | 1 |
| **Streaky bacon, chopped** | 1 oz | 25g | 2 tbsp |
| **Onion, chopped** | 1 | 1 | 1 |
| **Butter** | ½ oz | 15g | 1 tbsp |
| **Boneless turkey breasts, skinned** | 4 | 4 | 4 |
| **Salt and black pepper** | | | |
| **Chicken stock cube, crumbled** | 1 | 1 | 1 |
| **White wine, dry** | ½ pt | 300ml | 1¼ cups |
| **Can pimentos, drained and sliced** | 6¾ oz | 190g | small |
| **Cornflour (cornstarch)** | 1 tbsp | 1 tbsp | 1 tbsp |

*Method*
Choose a suitable deep container and rub the cut sides of the garlic round the inside of the container. Place the bacon and onion with the butter in the container, cover and cook for 4 minutes. Season the turkey breasts with salt and black pepper and add to the bacon and onion mixture. Sprinkle over the stock cube and add the wine. Cover and cook for 10 minutes. Stir in the drained pimentos, cover and cook for a further 5–10 minutes, depending on the size of the turkey breasts. Allow to stand for 15 minutes then arrange the turkey on a serving dish. Keep warm. Mix the cornflour with a little cold water to form a smooth paste and stir into the sauce. Cook for 2 minutes or until the sauce is thick (stir

once). Pour the sauce over the turkey and serve with crispy noodles and a green salad.

*Freezing:* Place the turkey in a freezer-to-microwave or polythene container, pour over the sauce, cool, cover, label and freeze.

## Duckling with Orange

| | Imp. | Met. | Am. |
|---|---|---|---|
| *Servings:* 4 | | *Cooking time:* 50 *mins* | |
| Duckling | 5 lb | 2·3kg | 5 lb |
| Onion, finely chopped | 1 | 1 | 1 |
| Butter | ½ oz | 15g | 1 tbsp |
| Cornflour (cornstarch) | 2 tbsp | 2 tbsp | 2 tbsp |
| Orange juice | ½ pt | 300ml | 1¼ cups |
| Rind of orange | 1 | 1 | 1 |
| To garnish: | | | |
| Orange segments or slices | | | |
| Watercress | | | |

*Method*
Use string to tie the legs and wings of the duckling before placing it in a roasting bag. Tie the opening with string (and do not forget to pierce the bag). Place an upturned saucer in a large shallow container and place the duckling on top, breast side down. Cook for 25 minutes. Drain off the fat and juices and put the bird back into the roasting bag. Cook for a further 20 minutes. Unwrap and place the duckling on a serving dish. Crisp the skin under a hot grill if desired.
Place the chopped onion and butter in a suitable bowl or jug, cover and cook for 2 minutes. Stir in the cornflour then gradually add the orange juice and rind, stirring continuously. Cook for 3 minutes, stirring every minute, until the sauce is thick. If liked, add some of the juices from the duckling. Pour a little sauce over the duckling and garnish with orange segments or slices and watercress. Serve the remaining sauce separately.

# 16

# Eggs and Cheese

Eggs and cheese are probably the most delicate foods to cook in the microwave oven. Timing is crucial for a few seconds can mean they are overcooked. A microwave oven may be compared to a high temperature conventional oven. It may be necessary, particularly when cooking eggs, to put an additional load, such as water, in the oven to absorb some of the energy. Microwaves do not penetrate eggs as easily as they penetrate other foods and occasionally the inner parts of an egg may remain liquid while the surfaces are well cooked.

Scrambled eggs are cooked superbly in a microwave oven – always creamy and smooth, and they need less attention than during conventional cooking. They can be cooked to just the right consistency to suit any taste.

Cooked egg dishes can be successfully reheated in the microwave oven in seconds.

I should like to stress that the following recipes are meant to *guide* the cook. Cooking times may need altering to suit your own oven. Cooking eggs and cheese is simpler if your oven has a turntable – more successful results are obtained with less attention. However, I suggest that you follow the manufacturer's recipes carefully for best results.

*Tips for cooking eggs and cheese*
Do not overcook, or the result will be tough and stringy. It is better to undercook and allow the dish to stand for a minute or two to let it finish cooking.

Best results are obtained if the eggs used are at room temperature.

Never try to cook an egg in its shell – pressure will build up inside and cause it to explode.

Follow manufacturers' instructions carefully when cooking eggs and cheese. Ovens and recipes vary and you will need to decide the best methods and times for your particular oven.

Cheese often requires only melting, so add it to a recipe near the end of the cooking time.

Grated cheese produces better results than chunks or slices.

Remember to turn the dish during cooking if your oven does not incorporate an automatic turntable.

## Baked Eggs

Butter the inside of a suitable saucer and crack an egg into this. Place the saucer in the microwave oven and cook for:
1 egg: 45 seconds
2 eggs: 1½ minutes
3 eggs: 2 minutes

## Scrambled Eggs

| *Servings:* 1 | | *Cooking time:* 1½ *mins* | |
|---|---|---|---|
| | *Imp.* | *Met.* | *Am.* |
| **Butter** | ½ oz | 15g | 1 tbsp |
| **Eggs** | 2 | 2 | 2 |
| **Milk** | 2 tbsp | 30ml | 2 tbsp |
| **Salt and pepper** | | | |

*Method*
Place the butter in a suitable container and cook for 15 seconds to melt. Beat in the remaining ingredients. Cook for about 1½ minutes, stirring after each 30 seconds. Stir well. Slightly undercook the eggs (they will continue cooking after they come out of the oven). Allow the eggs to stand for 1–2 minutes before serving on buttered toast.

*Variations:* Add one of the following before cooking – chopped chives, finely chopped onion, chopped parsley, your favourite herb.

## Cheese and Asparagus Flan

*Servings:* 4            *Cooking time:* 8 mins

| | *Imp.* | *Met.* | *Am.* |
|---|---|---|---|
| Cooked pastry case, 9 in (23cm) | 1 | 1 | 1 |
| Cheese, grated | 2 oz | 50g | 2 oz |
| Can asparagus | 12 oz | 340g | medium |
| Eggs, beaten | 3 | 3 | 3 |
| Carton single (thin) cream | 6 fl oz | 170ml | small |
| Salt and pepper | | | |

*Method*
Preferably the pastry case should have been cooked in a dish suitable for use in the microwave oven. If it is cooked in the microwave oven, prick the pastry first and cook for 4–5 minutes. Sprinkle the grated cheese over the base of the pastry case. Drain the asparagus and arrange on top of the cheese, stalks to the centre, tips to the outer edge. Beat together the eggs and cream and season to taste. Pour over the cheese and asparagus. Cook for 4 minutes then allow the flan to stand in the oven for 5 minutes. Cook for a further 4 minutes. Allow the flan to stand for 10 minutes before serving.

## Bacon and Mushroom Omelette

*Servings:* 2            *Cooking time:* 6½ mins

| | *Imp.* | *Met.* | *Am.* |
|---|---|---|---|
| Bacon rashers (slices), chopped | 2 | 2 | 2 |
| Mushrooms, chopped | 2 oz | 50g | 2 oz |
| Onion, chopped finely | 1 tbsp | 1 tbsp | 1 tbsp |
| Eggs | 4 | 4 | 4 |
| Milk | 4 tbsp | 60ml | 4 tbsp |
| Salt and pepper | | | |
| Butter | ½ oz | 15g | 1 tbsp |

*Method*
Place the bacon, mushrooms and onion in a suitable deep container. Cover and cook for 3 minutes, stirring once. Put

on one side. Beat together the eggs, milk and seasoning to taste. Place the butter in a suitable shallow dish (about 9 in/23cm diameter). Cook for 30 seconds or until the butter has melted. Tilt the dish so that the base is coated with melted butter. Pour the egg mixture into the dish. Cover and cook for 1½ minutes. Using a fork or spatula, move the cooked egg towards the centre of the dish. Cover and cook for a further 1½ minutes. Allow the omelette to stand for 1½ minutes then spread the bacon mixture over. Fold the omelette in half using a spatula and place on a serving dish. If the omelette is not quite cooked or needs reheating, put it back into the microwave oven and cook for ½–1 minute.

*Variations:* Cheese – sprinkle grated cheese on the omelette before allowing it to stand.

Onion, potato, peppers, tomatoes – any mixture cooked in the microwave oven before cooking the egg mixture.

Ham and parsley – sprinkle chopped cooked ham and chopped parsley on the omelette before allowing it to stand. Reheat before serving.

Pizza omelette – a cooked pizza topping prepared in the microwave oven beforehand (e.g. onion, mushrooms, bacon, tomato purée, herbs and seasoning) can be spread over the top of the cooked eggs. Do not fold the omelette but sprinkle with grated cheese and brown under a hot grill. Eat hot or serve cold in wedges.

## Swiss Fondue

| *Servings:* 4–6 | | *Cooking time:* 6 mins | |
|---|---|---|---|
| | *Imp.* | *Met.* | *Am.* |
| Garlic clove, halved | 1 | 1 | 1 |
| Swiss Emmenthal cheese, grated | 8 oz | 225g | ½ lb |
| Swiss Gruyere cheese, grated | 8 oz | 225g | ½ lb |
| Cornflour (cornstarch) | 2 tbsp | 2 tbsp | 2 tbsp |
| Salt and white pepper | | | |
| Ground nutmeg | pinch | pinch | pinch |
| Dry white wine | ½ pt | 300ml | 1¼ cups |
| Crusty bread, cut into cubes | | | |

*Method*

Rub the inside of a suitable container with the cut sides of the garlic clove, then discard them. In this dish mix together the cheeses, cornflour, seasoning and nutmeg. Pour the wine over and mix well. Cover and cook for 6 minutes, stirring twice during cooking. If the cheese is not completely melted, heat again for 30 seconds. Continue this until the fondue is creamy.

Serve in the cooking dish, dipping in cubes of crusty bread speared on long forks. If necessary the fondue may be returned to the microwave oven for reheating during the serving period.

## Hot Savoury Sandwich

*Serving:* 1                                   *Cooking time:* 1½ *mins*

|  | Imp. | Met. | Am. |
|---|---|---|---|
| Bread slices | 2 | 2 | 2 |
| Butter | ½ oz | 15g | 1 tbsp |
| Mustard, made up | 1 tsp | 1 tsp | 1 tsp |
| Cheese, sliced thinly | 2 oz | 50g | 2 oz |
| Tomato, sliced thinly | 1 | 1 | 1 |

*Method*

Spread one side of each bread slice with the butter and then the mustard. Place one slice, buttered side up, on a suitable plate and arrange the cheese and tomato on top. Put the other bread slice on top, buttered side down. Cook uncovered for 1½ minutes. This sandwich is delicious for breakfast and easy to eat with a knife and fork.

*Variations:* Try any of your favourite fillings suitable for a hot snack.

# 17

## VEGETABLES

If you enjoy eating vegetables which are slightly crisp and full of their natural flavour, then cooking with microwaves is for you. The colour, texture and flavour of vegetables cooked in a microwave oven will surprise you. Most fresh vegetables can be cooked with just 2–3 tbsp (30–45ml) of water and a little seasoning; and cooking vegetables speedily in a small amount of liquid must mean maximum retention of nutrients.

Reheating cooked vegetables is most successful too. Canned and frozen vegetables are reheated and cooked easily in a microwave oven.

Whole potatoes can be cooked in their skins in minutes;

the flavour and texture of microwave-cooked Ratatouille is perfect; and try cooking cabbage in your microwave oven – it is delicious (Smoky Cabbage, page 103).

It is possible to blanch vegetables in the microwave oven ready for freezing. Check with your manufacturer's instruction book for details. Generally, prepare the vegetables as for conventional blanching. Place the vegetables and water (about 3 fl oz/75ml per 1 lb/500g of vegetables) in a large container, cover and cook for about 4–6 minutes. Stir the vegetables once during blanching. Allow the vegetables to stand for one minute before cooling in iced water. Best results are obtained if small quantities only are prepared at one time.

*Tips for cooking vegetables*

Cooking times will depend on the type, age and quality of the vegetables, as well as the quantity being cooked. Your manufacturer's instruction book will be the best guide to cooking times and quantities of liquid required for your particular oven. Do use the recipes in this section as guides to average cooking times.

Cover all vegetables to be cooked or reheated in a microwave oven. This assists even cooking. The cover should be loose though, to allow steam to escape.

Stir the vegetables at least once during cooking. If your microwave oven does not have a turntable you will need to turn the dish several times during cooking.

Do not overcook vegetables or they will dry up very quickly. It is better to undercook since they will go on cooking after removal from the microwave oven.

Vegetables to be cooked in their skins should be pricked to allow steam to escape and to prevent them from splitting open during cooking.

Seasoning may be added before cooking but salt should be used sparingly or it will dry up the surface of the vegetables. It can be added later.

Do not try to cook too many whole potatoes at one time. You will find it speedier to do them in batches and the result will be a more evenly cooked vegetable.

To heat canned vegetables, drain off the liquid and heat in a covered container for a few minutes.

*Thawing vegetables*
Frozen raw vegetables need no thawing before cooking. Thawing and cooking are speedily completed simultaneously.

Frozen vegetables usually need no extra water to cook them. Assist cooking by removing any large pieces of ice.

Cooked vegetable recipes which have been frozen can be thawed quickly and reheated in the microwave oven. Stir or shake the covered container during the operation to assist even heating.

## Parsley Baked Onions

*Servings:* 4      *Cooking time:* 10–12 *mins*

| | Imp. | Met. | Am. |
|---|---|---|---|
| Onions, small, peeled, whole | ¾ lb | 350g | ¾ lb |
| Salt and black pepper | | | |
| Lemon juice | 1 tsp | 5ml | 1 tsp |
| Butter | 1½ oz | 40g | 3 tbsp |
| Parsley, chopped | 3 tbsp | 3 tbsp | 3 tbsp |

*Method*
Place all ingredients into a suitable container. Cover and cook for 10–12 minutes, depending on the size of the onions. Stir at least twice during cooking. Allow to stand for 10 minutes before serving.

## Pink Salad

*Servings:* 4              *Cooking time:* 15 *mins*

| | Imp. | Met. | Am. |
|---|---|---|---|
| Beetroot, skinned, diced, raw | 8 oz | 225g | ½ lb |
| White wine vinegar | 2 tbsp | 30ml | 2 tbsp |
| Water | 4 tbsp | 60ml | 4 tbsp |
| Sugar | 1 tsp | 1 tsp | 1 tsp |
| Celery stalks, sliced finely | 2 | 2 | 2 |
| Apples, peeled, cored and diced | 8 oz | 225g | ½ lb |

*Method*
Place the beetroot, vinegar, water and sugar into a suitable container, cover and cook for 15 minutes. Stir twice during cooking. Allow to stand for 10 minutes then stir in the celery and apples. Chill well before serving with cold meat or fish.

*Freezing:* Pack into a foil or polythene container, cool, cover, label and freeze.

## Carrots with Orange

*Servings:* 4              *Cooking time:* 10 *mins*

| | Imp. | Met. | Am. |
|---|---|---|---|
| Carrots, sliced finely | 1 lb | 450g | 1 lb |
| Water | 5 tbsp | 75ml | 5 tbsp |
| Butter | 1 oz | 25g | 2 tbsp |
| Salt and black pepper | | | |
| Orange juice | 2 tbsp | 30ml | 2 tbsp |
| Parsley, chopped | 1 tbsp | 1 tbsp | 1 tbsp |

*Method*
Place the carrots in a suitable container and pour over the water. Add the butter and season to taste. Cover and cook for 10 minutes, stirring twice during cooking. Drain the carrots if necessary and stir in the orange juice and parsley before serving.

# Buttered Marrow

*Servings:* 4–6           *Cooking time:* 10 *mins*

| | Imp. | Met. | Am. |
|---|---|---|---|
| Marrow, deseeded and cut into cubes | 1 lb | 450g | 1 lb |
| Water | 1 tbsp | 15ml | 1 tbsp |
| Butter | 1½ oz | 40g | 3 tbsp |
| Salt | | | |
| Black pepper | | | |

*Method*

Mix together all the ingredients in a suitable container. Cover and cook for 10 minutes, stirring twice during cooking. Allow to stand for 5 minutes before serving.

*Variation:* Sprinkle with grated cheese mixed with a little chopped parsley and brown under a hot grill. Good as a starter or an accompaniment to meat or fish.

# Cauliflower in Piquant Sauce

*Servings:* 4           *Cooking time:* 13–14 *mins*

| | Imp. | Met. | Am. |
|---|---|---|---|
| Medium cauliflower, cut into florets | 1 | 1 | 1 |
| Water | 2 tbsp | 30ml | 2 tbsp |
| Salt | | | |
| Butter | 1 oz | 25g | 2 tbsp |
| Flour | 1 oz | 25g | ¼ cup |
| Black pepper | | | |
| English mustard, made up | 2 tsp | 2 tsp | 2 tsp |
| Milk | ½ pt | 300ml | 1¼ cups |
| Parsley, chopped | 1 tbsp | 1 tbsp | 1 tbsp |
| Parmesan cheese | | | |

*Method*

Place the cauliflower florets and water in a suitable container. Sprinkle with salt, cover and cook for 8 minutes, stirring once. Set to one side. Place the butter in a suitable bowl or jug. Heat for 30 seconds or until melted. Blend in the flour and season with salt and black pepper. Add the mustard then gradually stir in the milk. Cook for 4 minutes, stirring every minute, until the sauce is thick and smooth. Pour the sauce over the cauliflower and sprinkle over the parsley and some Parmesan cheese. Cook for 1 minute so that the cauliflower is heated through.

*Variation:* The sauce may be flavoured with cheese, fresh or dried herbs, capers, or with sauces such as Worcestershire or horseradish to replace the mustard.


## Ratatouille

| Servings: 4–6 | | Cooking time: 20 mins | |
|---|---|---|---|
| | Imp. | Met. | Am. |
| Aubergines, sliced | 8 oz | 225g | ½ lb |
| Cooking oil | 3 tbsp | 45ml | 3 tbsp |
| Garlic clove, crushed | 1 | 1 | 1 |
| Onions, sliced finely | 8 oz | 225g | ½ lb |
| Courgettes (squash), sliced | 8 oz | 225g | ½ lb |
| Green pepper, deseeded, sliced finely | 1 | 1 | 1 |
| Red pepper, deseeded, sliced finely | 1 | 1 | 1 |
| Tomatoes, skinned, sliced thickly | 1 lb | 450g | 1 lb |
| Basil | 1 tsp | 1 tsp | 1 tsp |
| Salt and black pepper | | | |

*Method*
Sprinkle the sliced aubergines lightly with salt and leave for 20–30 minutes. Rinse under cold water, draining well. Place the cooking oil, garlic and onions into a suitable deep container. Cover and cook for 5 minutes. Stir in the aubergines, courgettes and peppers, cover and cook for 5 minutes. Add the tomatoes and basil. Season well with salt and pepper. Cover and cook for a further 10 minutes, stirring twice during cooking.
Serve hot or cold as a starter or as a vegetable accompanying meats, fish, salad etc.

*Freezing:* Place in a freezer-to-microwave or polythene container, cool, cover, label and freeze.

# Smoky Cabbage

*Servings:* 4                          *Cooking time:* 14 *mins*

|                              | Imp.   | Met.  | Am.    |
| ---------------------------- | ------ | ----- | ------ |
| Cabbage, shredded finely     | 1 lb   | 450g  | 1 lb   |
| Water                        | 3 tbsp | 45ml  | 3 tbsp |
| Butter                       | 1 oz   | 25g   | 2 tbsp |
| Salt and pepper              |        |       |        |
| Bacon rashers (slices), smoked streaky | 4 | 4 | 4 |

*Method*
Place the cabbage in a suitable deep container and pour over the water. Place the butter on top, cover and cook for 10 minutes, stirring after 5 minutes. Set to one side.
Place the bacon rashers between two sheets of kitchen paper on a suitable plate. Cook for at least 4 minutes or until the bacon is crisp. Chop finely or crumble and sprinkle over the cabbage to serve.

# Potatoes with Parsley Cream

*Servings:* 4                          *Cooking time:* 12 *mins*

|                              | Imp.     | Met.   | Am.     |
| ---------------------------- | -------- | ------ | ------- |
| Potatoes, peeled and sliced  | 1½ lb    | 700g   | 1½ lb   |
| Water                        | 2 tbsp   | 30ml   | 2 tbsp  |
| Salt and pepper              |          |        |         |
| Cornflour (cornstarch)       | 2 tsp    | 2 tsp  | 2 tsp   |
| Top of milk                  | ¼ pt     | 150ml  | ⅔ cup   |
| Butter                       | ½ oz     | 15g    | 1 tbsp  |
| Parsley, chopped             | 1 tbsp   | 1 tbsp | 1 tbsp  |

*Method*
Place the potatoes and water in a suitable deep container, seasoning each layer lightly with salt and pepper. Cover and cook for 10 minutes, stirring once. Set on one side for 5–10 minutes. Mix the cornflour with a little of the cold milk to form a smooth paste. Dot the butter on top and sprinkle over the parsley. Cook for 2 minutes, stirring frequently, or until the sauce is thick and smooth. Stir into the cooked

potatoes and reheat if necessary. This dish is attractive if browned under a hot grill for a few minutes.

*Freezing:* Place in a freezer-to-microwave or polythene container, cool, cover, label and freeze.

*Variations:* Replace the parsley with chives, your favourite dried herb, or mustard.

## Courgette and Mushroom Cream

*Servings:* 4          *Cooking time:* 14–16 *mins*

| | Imp. | Met. | Am. |
|---|---|---|---|
| Celery stick (stalk) chopped finely | 1 | 1 | 1 |
| Onion, chopped finely | 1 | 1 | 1 |
| Butter | 1 oz | 25g | 2 tbsp |
| Courgettes (squash), sliced | 1 lb | 450g | 1 lb |
| Can condensed mushroom soup | 10½ oz | 298g | medium |
| Salt and pepper | | | |
| Chives, chopped | 1 tbsp | 1 tbsp | 1 tbsp |
| Mushrooms, sliced and fried | 2 oz | 50g | 2 oz |

*Method*
Place the celery, onion and butter in a suitable deep container, cover and cook for 4 minutes, stirring once. Add the courgettes, mushroom soup and seasoning and mix together well. Cover and cook for 10–12 minutes, stirring once. The courgettes should have a slight bite. Allow to stand for 5–10 minutes before serving.
To serve, stir in the chives and sprinkle over the fried mushroom slices. Delicious with roast meats.

*Freezing:* Place in a freezer-to-microwave or polythene container, cool, cover, label and freeze.

# Savoury Baked Potatoes

*Servings:* 4 *Cooking time:* 10–15 *mins*

| | Imp. | Met. | Am. |
|---|---|---|---|
| Potatoes, weighing about 6 oz/175g each, scrubbed | 4 | 4 | 4 |
| Milk | 3 tbsp | 45ml | 3 tbsp |
| Cheese, grated | 2 oz | 50g | ½ cup |
| Mustard powder | ½ tsp | ½ tsp | ½ tsp |
| Butter | 1 oz | 25g | 2 tbsp |
| Chives, chopped *or* parsley, chopped | 2 tbsp | 2 tbsp | 2 tbsp |
| Salt and pepper | | | |

*Method*
Prick the potatoes well with a fork. Space the potatoes evenly on the microwave oven shelf. Cook for 10–15 minutes, taking out any potato that is cooked. Allow to stand for 5–10 minutes. Split the potatoes on one side and scoop out their centres. Mix together with the remaining ingredients. Pack the mixture back into the potato skins and reheat in the microwave oven if necessary. It may be easier to wrap the potatoes in foil before splitting but *do not* then put them back into the microwave oven.
*Variations:* Replace the cheese and chives with your favourite herb, or any cooked, flaked fish. Alternatively, simply cook the potatoes as instructed and serve, split, with butter.

# 18

# Rice, Pasta and Cereals

Cooking rice and pasta in a microwave oven is possible but it takes almost as long as cooking conventionally. The microwave oven is however ideal for reheating them quickly and successfully – a big advantage if ever you have tried to separate badly heated grains of rice or lumps of spaghetti.

Cereals, such as semolina or oat breakfast cereals, are prepared in the microwave oven with little effort. Simply place the cereal in its serving bowl, stir in the liquid and cook for one or two minutes in the microwave oven. Stir well before serving. When preparing large quantities of cereal, use a large container, cover loosely and stir several times during cooking. Some cereals benefit from a little standing time to allow for thickening. Reheating cereals is quick too.

Remember, if your oven has no turntable, to turn the container once or twice during cooking or reheating.

*Tips for cooking rice and pasta*

The dish should be large enough to contain the rice/pasta and water without it boiling over.

The container should be covered lightly to allow steam to escape.

Check with your instruction book for cooking times and the amount of liquid to use. Make sure that pasta is completely immersed in the cooking liquid or it will become brown and brittle.

After cooking allow the covered container to stand for about 10 minutes. After standing fluff up rice with a fork.

To reheat rice, spaghetti, macaroni, or noodles, place in a suitable container (*do not* add water) cover loosely and heat in the microwave oven until it steams.

*Thawing rice*
Frozen rice dishes are simply defrosted in a microwave oven.
The container should be covered and the rice broken up with
a fork during the thawing period. Allow to stand for a few
minutes before serving. If the dish is required hot, reheat in
the microwave oven.

## Rice

*Servings:* 4                          *Cooking time:* 14 *mins*

|                 | Imp.    | Met.   | Am.    |
|-----------------|---------|--------|--------|
| Rice, long grain | 6 oz   | 175g   | 1 cup  |
| Water           | ¾ pt    | 400ml  | 2 cups |
| Butter          | ½ oz    | 15g    | 1 tbsp |
| Salt            | 1 tsp   | 1 tsp  | 1 tsp  |

*Method*
Place all the ingredients in a suitable deep container. Cover
and cook for 14 minutes. Allow to stand for 5 minutes
before fluffing up with a fork to serve. If the rice is not quite
cooked after standing, return the covered container to the
microwave oven and cook for a further few minutes.

## Macaroni

*Servings:* 4                          *Cooking time:* 15 *mins*

|                 | Imp.    | Met.    | Am.    |
|-----------------|---------|---------|--------|
| Macaroni        | 8 oz    | 225g    | 2 cups |
| Water, boiling  | 1¾ pt   | 1 litre | 4 cups |
| Salt            | 1 tsp   | 1 tsp   | 1 tsp  |

*Method*
Pour the boiling water over the macaroni in a suitable deep
container and stir. Cover and cook for 15 minutes or until
cooked. Drain before serving, perhaps with a knob of
butter and some chopped parsley.

## Rice Pilaff

*Servings:* 4           *Cooking time:* 13 *mins*

|  | Imp. | Met. | Am. |
|---|---|---|---|
| Butter | 2 oz | 50g | 4 tbsp |
| Onion, chopped finely | 4 tbsp | 4 tbsp | 4 tbsp |
| Celery, chopped finely | 4 tbsp | 4 tbsp | 4 tbsp |
| Long grain rice | 4 oz | 100g | ¼ lb |
| Chicken stock | ¾ pt | 400ml | 2 cups |
| Salt and pepper | | | |
| Parsley, chopped | 2 tbsp | 2 tbsp | 2 tbsp |

*Method*
Place the butter, onion and celery in a suitable container.
Cook covered for 3 minutes. Add the rice, stock and seasoning to taste. Cook uncovered for 10 minutes. Stir quickly
then allow to stand for 5–10 minutes until the liquid has
been absorbed. Stir in the parsley before serving. Reheat in
the microwave oven if necessary. Serve with cooked meat.

*Freezing:* Omit parsley. Pack into a freezer-to-microwave or
polythene container, cool, cover, label and freeze.

## Porridge

*Servings:* 4           *Cooking time:* 7 *mins*

|  | Imp. | Met. | Am. |
|---|---|---|---|
| Water | 1 pt | 550ml | 2½ cups |
| Porridge oats | 4 oz | 100g | ¼ lb |
| Salt | 1 tsp | 1 tsp | 1 tsp |

*Method*
Mix together the three ingredients in a suitable deep container. Cover and cook for 7 minutes, stirring at least three
times during cooking. Stir before serving with milk, sugar,
honey, salt, etc.

    To make an individual serving: Place 1 oz/25g/2 tbsp of
oats in a bowl with ¼ pt/150ml/⅔ cup of water and a pinch of
salt. Cover and cook for 2 minutes. Stir well. Allow to stand
1 minute before serving.

# Lasagne

| | *Imp.* | *Met.* | *Am.* |
|---|---|---|---|
| *Servings:* 4 | | *Cooking time:* 24 mins | |
| **Meat sauce:** | | | |
| Onion, chopped | 1 | 1 | 1 |
| Garlic clove, crushed | 1 | 1 | 1 |
| Butter | ½ oz | 15g | 1 tbsp |
| Cooking oil | 1 tbsp | 15ml | 1 tbsp |
| Minced beef, lean | 4 oz | 100g | ¼ lb |
| Tomato purée (paste) | 3 tbsp | 3 tbsp | 3 tbsp |
| Beef stock (bouillon) | ¼ pt | 150ml | ⅔ cup |
| Bay leaf | 1 | 1 | 1 |
| Oregano | 1 tsp | 1 tsp | 1 tsp |
| Salt and pepper | | | |
| **Cheese sauce:** | | | |
| Butter | 1 oz | 25g | 2 tbsp |
| Flour | 1 oz | 25g | ¼ cup |
| Mustard powder | ½ tsp | ½ tsp | ½ tsp |
| Milk | ½ pt | 300ml | 1¼ cups |
| Cheese, grated | 2 oz | 50g | 2 oz |
| Butter | 1 oz | 25g | 2 tbsp |
| Lasagne leaves, quick-cook | 4 oz | 100g | ¼ lb |

## Method

Place the onion, garlic, butter and cooking oil into a suitable container, cover and cook for 3 minutes. Stir in the beef, cover and cook for 3 minutes, stirring once. Add the tomato purée, stock, bay leaf, oregano and seasoning. Cover and cook for 4 minutes, stirring once. Allow to stand for 5 minutes. Remove bay leaf.

To make the cheese sauce, place the butter in a suitable bowl or jug. Cook for 30 seconds to melt. Stir in the flour and mustard then gradually add the milk, stirring well. Season with salt and pepper. Cook for 3 minutes, stirring every minute, until the sauce is thick. Stir in 1 oz/25g of the cheese.

To prepare the lasagne, place the butter in a suitable small bowl. Cook for 30 seconds to melt. Brush the uncooked lasagne with the melted butter.

Spread some of the meat in the bottom of a suitable container, then cover with a layer of pasta. Spread some cheese sauce on the pasta. Continue making these layers, ending with cheese sauce. Sprinkle the remaining cheese over the top. Cook uncovered for 10 minutes then brown the top of the finished lasagne under a hot grill.

*Freezing:* Best frozen in the cooking container. Cool, cover, label and freeze.

# 19

# Fruit and Desserts

The great advantage of thawing, heating or cooking fruit (fresh or frozen) in a microwave oven is that it retains its flavour, its colour and particularly its shape. In fact it is cooked to perfection. Your favourite fruits will have even more appeal than previously. Additionally, speedy cooking in the minimum amount of liquid means that nutrients are retained.

Use the microwave oven to bring refrigerated fruits quickly to room temperature for eating.

All sorts of puddings and desserts can be prepared using microwaves. Puddings, custards, cheesecakes, mousses and crumbles are just some. Thawing puddings and other desserts is simple too and they may be cooked or reheated quickly, either whole or as individual portions. So it is possible to prepare a variety of desserts in single portions in less time than it would take to make one conventionally.

*Tips for cooking fruit*
Again the rule is to undercook – the fruit will go on cooking after removal from the microwave oven.

Place the prepared fruit with or without sugar and flavourings, into a suitable container. Cover the container lightly (to allow steam to escape).

Stir fruit once during cooking to ensure that it cooks evenly. If your oven does not incorporate a turntable, you will need to turn or rotate the dish frequently during cooking.

Cooking times will vary according to the type of fruit, its age, the quantity being cooked, its temperature, and the method of preparation (whole, sliced etc.). Check with your instruction book.

A general guide would be:  soft fruits  2½–5 minutes
hard fruits  7–10 minutes

Fruits to be cooked in their skins, such as apples, should be pricked or cut to avoid splitting during cooking.

## Thawing fruits

No extra liquid is necessary when thawing frozen fruits. There will be sufficient moisture from the melting ice. You will be amazed at the speed of thawing, so do not heat for too long and check the thawing fruit often. It should be left to finish thawing after it is removed from the microwave oven. During thawing, separate the fruit carefully with a fork. This will assist even heat penetration.

## Tips for cooking puddings and desserts

The shape and size of the container to be used will depend entirely on the type of pudding or dessert being prepared. Your manufacturer's recipe book will provide you with a vast choice of recipes, all with different requirements and cooking times too numerous to list here.

Generally, the container should be covered where moisture is to be retained.

## Thawing puddings and desserts

Best results are obtained if the pudding or dessert is subjected to short bursts of microwave energy with rests between (easy if your oven has an automatic defrost setting).

Take care not to heat the dish for too long. The defrosting time of a sponge-type pudding for instance is very short. It is better to allow the pudding to go on thawing after it is removed from the microwave oven.

# Honey Baked Bananas

*Servings:* 4            *Cooking time:* 6 mins

|  | Imp. | Met. | Am. |
| --- | --- | --- | --- |
| Butter | 1 oz | 25g | 2 tbsp |
| Juice of orange | 1 | 1 | 1 |
| Honey, clear preferable | 1 tbsp | 1 tbsp | 1 tbsp |
| Bananas | 4 | 4 | 4 |

## Method

Place the butter, orange juice and honey in a suitable shallow container, cover and cook for 2 minutes until the mixture has melted. Stir well then add the bananas, skinned and halved lengthways. Cover the bananas with the honey mixture. Cover and cook for 3–4 minutes, depending on the size and ripeness of the bananas. Serve immediately with cream or custard sauce.

*Variations:* the orange juice may be replaced with lemon juice or sherry or a liqueur.

## Plum and Walnut Compote

| Servings: 4 | Imp. | Cooking time: 5 mins Met. | Am. |
|---|---|---|---|
| Plums, halved and stoned | 1 lb | 450g | 1 lb |
| Demerara (brown) sugar | 1 oz | 25g | 2 tbsp |
| Walnuts, chopped roughly | 1 oz | 25g | 2 tbsp |
| Sherry flavouring, *or* | 1 tsp | 5 ml | 1 tsp |
| medium sherry | 1–2 tbsp | 15–30ml | 1–2 tbsp |

### Method
Mix together all the ingredients in a suitable container. Cover and cook for 5 minutes, stirring once. Serve hot or cold with cream, custard sauce or ice cream. This mixture is also suitable for use as a pie filling or a crumble base.

*Freezing:* Pack into a freezer-to-microwave or polythene container, cool, cover, label and freeze.

*Variations:* Any nuts may be used to replace the walnuts. Try using desiccated coconut for a change.

## Blackberry and Apple Shortbread

| Servings: 6 | Imp. | Cooking time: 13 mins Met. | Am. |
|---|---|---|---|
| Blackberries | 12 oz | 350g | ¾ lb |
| Apples, peeled, cored and sliced | 8 oz | 225g | ½ lb |
| Sugar | 1 oz | 25g | 2 tbsp |
| Shortbread: | | | |
| Butter | 8 oz | 225g | ½ lb |

## Blackberry and Apple Shortbread—contd.

| | | | |
|---|---|---|---|
| Caster (superfine) sugar | 4 oz | 100g | ¼ lb |
| Flour, plain | 10 oz | 275g | 2½ cups |
| Fine semolina | 2 oz | 50g | 2 oz |

To decorate:
Caster (superfine) sugar
Whipped cream

*Method*
Place the blackberries, apples and sugar into a suitable container. Cover and cook for 5 minutes. Allow to cool.
Shortbread: Cream together the butter and the sugar until light and fluffy. Sieve the flour and semolina and fold gently into the butter mixture. Knead lightly to form a dough. Divide into two and press each half into an equal sized greased container (about 6 in/15cm diameter). Cook each half in the microwave oven for 4 minutes. Cut one circle into 6 segments while still warm. Sprinkle with caster sugar and allow to cool.
To serve: Place the whole shortbread circle on a serving dish and spread the blackberry and apple mixture over it. Arrange the shortbread pieces on top then decorate with caster sugar and whipped cream.

*Freezing:* Freeze the blackberry mixture and the shortbread separately. Assemble when thawed then decorate as above.

*Variations:* Any fruit may replace the blackberry and apple. Try using a can of pie filling.

## Rhubarb and Orange Crumble

*Servings:* 4  *Cooking time:* 9 *mins*

| | Imp. | Met. | Am. |
|---|---|---|---|
| Rhubarb, cut into 1 in/ 2½cm lengths | 1 lb | 450g | 1 lb |
| Orange juice | 2–3 tbsp | 30–45ml | 2–3 tbsp |
| Sugar, brown | 1–2 oz | 25–50g | 2–3 tbsp |

**Crumble:**

| | Imp. | Met. | Am. |
|---|---|---|---|
| Butter or margarine | 2 oz | 50g | 2 oz |
| Flour, plain | 4 oz | 100g | 1 cup |
| Caster (superfine) sugar | 1 oz | 25g | 2 tbsp |

*Method*

Place the rhubarb, orange juice and sugar into a suitable container, cover and cook for 5 minutes, stirring once.
Crumble: In a bowl, rub the butter into the flour until the mixture resembles fine breadcrumbs. Stir in the sugar. Spread the mixture over the rhubarb. Cook uncovered for 4 minutes. Sprinkle with a little brown sugar to serve, or brown lightly under a hot grill. Serve with cream or custard sauce.

*Variations:* Substitute any cooked fresh fruit for the rhubarb, or use a can of pie filling.

## Baked Apples

*Servings:* 4

*Cooking time:* 5 mins

| | Imp. | Met. | Am. |
|---|---|---|---|
| Cooking apples, cored | 4 | 4 | 4 |
| Demerara sugar | 4 tbsp | 4 tbsp | 4 tbsp |
| Raisins | 4 tbsp | 4 tbsp | 4 tbsp |
| Currants | 1 tbsp | 1 tbsp | 1 tbsp |
| Ground almonds | 1 tsp | 1 tsp | 1 tsp |
| Cinnamon | 1 tsp | 1 tsp | 1 tsp |
| Water | 4 tbsp | 60ml | 4 tbsp |

*Method*

Score the apples once around the middle with a sharp knife and arrange them on a suitable large, shallow container. Mix together the sugar, raisins, currants, ground almonds and cinnamon. Fill each apple well with this mixture. Scatter any remaining mixture around the apples. Cover and cook for about 5 minutes, depending on the size of the apples. Stand for 5–10 minutes before serving. Serve with cream or custard sauce.

## Pears in Cider

*Servings:* 4                        *Cooking time:* 10 *mins*

|  | Imp. | Met. | Am. |
| --- | --- | --- | --- |
| Pears, small, peeled | 8 | 8 | 8 |
| Demerara sugar | 2 tbsp | 2 tbsp | 2 tbsp |
| Sweet cider | ½ pt | 300ml | 1¼ cups |
| Vanilla essence | 1 tsp | 5ml | 1 tsp |

*Method*
Place the whole pears upright in a suitable large container. Mix together the remaining ingredients and use to coat the pears. Cover and cook for 10 minutes, basting the pears twice during cooking. Serve hot or chilled with cream.

*Variation:* Try cooking the pears in a red wine instead of cider.

## Golden Pudding

*Servings:* 4                        *Cooking time:* 6 *mins*

|  | Imp. | Met. | Am. |
| --- | --- | --- | --- |
| Golden syrup | 2 tbsp | 2 tbsp | 2 tbsp |
| Margarine | 2 oz | 50g | ¼ cup |
| Caster (superfine) sugar | 2 oz | 50g | 4 tbsp |
| Self-raising flour (flour with ½ tsp baking powder) | 2 oz | 50g | ½ cup |
| Egg, beaten lightly | 1 | 1 | 1 |
| Almond essence | ½ tsp | ½ tsp | ½ tsp |

*Method*
Lightly grease a suitable pie dish and spread the golden syrup over the base. Beat together the remaining ingredients and spread the mixture over the syrup. Cover and cook for 6 minutes. Allow the pudding to stand for 5 minutes before turning out and serving. Serve with cream or custard sauce.

*Freezing:* Best frozen in the cooking container. Cool, cover, label and freeze.

# Egg Custard

*Servings:* 4      *Cooking time:* 9½ mins

| | Imp. | Met. | Am. |
|---|---|---|---|
| Milk | 1 pt | 550ml | 2½ cups |
| Eggs, beaten lightly | 4 | 4 | 4 |
| Caster (superfine) sugar | 1 oz | 25g | 2 tbsp |
| Vanilla essence | 3 drops | 3 drops | 3 drops |
| Ground nutmeg | | | |

*Method*
Pour the milk into a large suitable container. Cook for 3½ minutes. Meanwhile, beat together the eggs, sugar and vanilla essence in a suitable container. Pour the warmed milk on to the egg mixture and stir. Sprinkle some nutmeg over the top. Cover and cook for 6 minutes. Allow to stand for 5–10 minutes before serving. The custard is cooked when a knife inserted in the centre comes out clean.

# Orange and Lemon Cheesecake

*Servings:* 4      *Cooking time:* 2 mins

| | Imp. | Met. | Am. |
|---|---|---|---|
| Butter | 2 oz | 50g | 4 tbsp |
| Dark brown sugar | 1 oz | 25g | 2 tbsp |
| Digestive biscuits, crushed | 4 oz | 100g | ¼ lb |
| Full fat cream cheese | 12 oz | 350g | ¾ lb |
| Caster (superfine) sugar | 3 oz | 75g | 6 tbsp |
| Grated rind and juice of lemon | 1 | 1 | 1 |
| Grated rind and juice of orange | 1 | 1 | 1 |
| Cold water | 2 tbsp | 30ml | 2 tbsp |
| Powdered gelatine | ½ oz | 15g | 1 pkt |
| Double (thick) cream | ¼ pt | 150ml | ⅔ cup |

To decorate:
Whipped cream
Orange segments
Lemon rind

## Method

Line an 8 in/20cm cake or flan tin with foil. Place the butter in a suitable bowl and cook for 1 minute to melt. Stir in the brown sugar and crumbled biscuits. Spread the mixture over the base and sides of the prepared cake tin. Refrigerate for about 30 minutes. Beat together the cheese, sugar, lemon and orange rind and juice until smooth. Place the water in a small bowl and sprinkle the gelatine over. Cook for 1 minute to dissolve the gelatine (but do not boil), then stir it into the cheese mixture. Whisk the cream until stiff and fold into the cheese mixture. Spread the mixture into the biscuit case. When set decorate with whipped cream, orange segments and small curls of lemon rind. To serve, lift the cheesecake out of its container, using the foil to help you, then simply peel off the foil.

*Freezing:* Open freeze. When frozen, remove the cake tin and wrap the cheesecake in foil. Omit orange segments and lemon peel.

## Chocolate and Orange Mousse

*Servings:* 4                         *Cooking time:* 2½ mins

|  | Imp. | Met. | Am. |
|---|---|---|---|
| Plain (dark) chocolate | 8 oz | 225g | ½ lb |
| Butter | 1½ oz | 40g | 3 tbsp |
| Eggs, separated | 4 | 4 | 4 |
| Frozen concentrated orange juice, defrosted | 2 tbsp | 30ml | 2 tbsp |

To decorate:
Whipped cream
Grated chocolate

## Method

Break the chocolate into a suitable bowl and add the butter. Cook for 2½ minutes to melt. Beat the mixture well and if necessary return it to the microwave oven for 15–30 seconds longer. Beat in the egg yolks then stir in the concentrated orange juice. Whisk the egg whites until stiff then fold them carefully into the chocolate mixture. Pour into a serving dish and refrigerate until set. Decorate with whipped cream and grated chocolate.

*Freezing:* Best frozen in the serving dish, covered with foil.

# 20

## CAKES & BISCUITS

### Cakes

Cake making, using the microwave oven, can be fascinating and most creative. Since almost any *non-metal* container can be used the choice of shapes can be endless. I have not included recipes for cakes in this book. I feel it is better to use your manufacturer's recipes which will have been developed for your particular oven. When you start experimenting with your own cake recipes it is worth remembering that they will probably need slight adjustments for microwave cooking. In general, moist mixtures are more successful than stiff ones. Rich cakes, containing a lot of dried fruit, do not cook well by microwaves. The raising agent in a conventional recipe should be reduced by up to a quarter for microwave cooking.

As a rule, the container should be lightly oiled or lined with greaseproof paper or cling film. Never flour the container or an unpalatable crust will form on the outside of the cake. Do not fill the container more than half full of uncooked cake mixture. You will be surprised how well cakes rise in a microwave oven.

If your oven does not have an automatic turntable it will be necessary to turn the cake in its container every couple of minutes. This helps the cake to rise evenly. Do not be afraid to open the oven door, the cake retains heat in a microwave oven and is unlikely to sink. It is better to cook one layer of a cake at a time rather than cooking two together.

After cooking allow the cake to stand for 10 minutes to go on cooking and rising in its container. Check that the cake is cooked by inserting a skewer into the centre. If it comes out clean the cake is cooked.

Though microwave-cooked cakes will not have the characteristic golden brown colour of conventional cooking, flavourings, colourings and icings, chocolate, etc., can easily be used to recreate the conventional appearance.

Use the microwave oven for thawing cakes too. A large cake (without cream – a cream cake does not thaw successfully; the cream defrosts before the cake) takes just a few minutes. Allow the cake to stand for 5 minutes before serving to allow its temperature to equalize. Small cakes will defrost in only a few seconds. Allow these to stand for 2 minutes before serving.

## Pastry

It will depend entirely on personal taste as to whether microwave-cooked pastry is acceptable. Best results are obtained cooking open flan cases before filling. Do not try to cook a pie with a top and bottom crust, the filling will bubble out before the pastry is cooked. Experience will soon be your best guide when cooking pastry. You may find it more convenient, and the result more acceptable (since it will brown), to cook pastry in the conventional way and reheat the made-up dish in the microwave oven. Cooked and filled

vol-au-vent cases and other pastry cases are heated successfully in the microwave oven.

Biscuit crust is prepared with little effort. Simply melt the
butter in the microwave oven and stir in the crushed biscuits.

Cooked frozen pies and tarts can be speedily thawed in
the microwave oven. Best results are obtained if the pastry is
subjected to short bursts of energy with rests between – easy
if your oven has an automatic defrost control. When heating
individual pies, turn the pie upside down in the microwave
oven. This way the steam from the filling does not soften the
top crust. The contents of a pie, whether mince, chicken,
meat, fruit etc., is heated in minutes. Beware though, the
contents are always much hotter than the pastry feels.

## Biscuits

Best results are obtained with mixtures which are cut into
shape after cooking. Your manufacturer will have included
specially developed recipes in your instruction book. Individual biscuits tend to spread during microwave cooking
and are not so successful. As with cakes, a golden brown
colour cannot be achieved. However, appearance can be
improved simply by careful use of flavouring, colourings
etc. Generally biscuits are cooked uncovered on a sheet of
greased greaseproof paper or a greased plate. Do not flour
the surface since this will result in a tough, floury crust.

Thaw frozen biscuits on a paper towel. The time will depend on the type of biscuit and the number being prepared.

## Confectionery

Sweet-making is easy in a microwave oven. A particular
advantage is that the risk of burning or scorching is reduced,
particularly when high temperatures are needed. Use an
uncovered container which will hold twice or three times the
quantity being prepared. Take care when handling the container after microwave cooking. It will be very hot. A sugar
thermometer may be used to check the mixture but *never*
leave it inside the microwave oven when it is switched on.
You will find a great selection of tempting sweet recipes in
your manufacturer's recipe book.

## Bread

It is possible to cook a variety of breads in the microwave oven. All rise well but they will not have the characteristic crisp crust or a browned appearance. Best results are obtained when the bread is uncovered during cooking. The container should be lightly greased or lined with greaseproof paper. Do not flour the container or a thick, floury crust will bake on to the outside of the bread. Since microwaves do not brown and crisp, you may like to cook the bread in the microwave oven then transfer it to a hot conventional oven for a few minutes.

Care should be taken not to overcook bread or it will become tough and rubbery. The centre will be hotter than the outer surfaces.

When reheating bread (perhaps to freshen it) place it on a piece of kitchen paper so that any moisture is absorbed.

Use the microwave oven to thaw frozen bread in minutes. Forget the days when you took a whole loaf out of the freezer 'just in case'. Bread can be taken out of the freezer when required – whole loaves, rolls, or even individual slices.

Frozen bread dough can also be thawed using microwaves. Bread-making then becomes a speedy operation since the dough may be proved in the microwave oven too.

The manufacturer's recipe book will give instructions on how to make various types of bread, how to reheat them, and how to thaw uncooked and cooked bread. The recipes will have been developed with your oven in mind so there will be little risk of failure.

## Beverages

These can be mixed, heated and served in the same container. Remember to use a cup or mug large enough to hold the drink without it boiling over, and do not cover those which have a tendency to boil over anyway (milk drinks for example).

Heating times will depend on the liquid, its temperature, and the size of the container. You will soon learn how long it takes to make a cup of coffee in your favourite mug. As a rough guide, one cup of water will take 1–1½ minutes. Try heating other drinks too: milk shakes, fruit drinks, mulled wine or cider (good for a party).

Thaw frozen drinks in your microwave oven. If the frozen juice is canned, remove the can before thawing. Place it in hot water for 1–2 minutes then empty the contents into a suitable container (open both ends and push the frozen block out). Thaw uncovered, stirring the juice once or twice.

*Finally, do not forget that a microwave oven can be used to:*

*Melt jelly cubes.* Break up the jelly into ½ pt/300ml/1¼ cups of water and heat for 2 minutes. Make up the jelly to 1 pint/ 550ml/2½ cups with cold water.

*Dissolve gelatine.* No need to do this laboriously in a basin sitting on a pan of hot water.

*Melt jam* to spread over a fruit cake before adding marzipan. Remove every scrap from a jam jar by heating the nearly empty jar in the microwave oven.

*Melt chocolate.* No need for careful heating over a pan of hot water. Simply place the broken chocolate in a suitable bowl and heat until melted (about 1 minute).

*Soften butter* or margarine from the refrigerator. 8 oz/225g/ ½ lb takes about 15 seconds and is ready for spreading or baking.

*Melt fats* in small amounts for brushing foods for grilling etc.

*Warm milk* in the bottle to 'tepid' or 'blood heat' before pouring on to eggs for custards, etc.

*Heat baby foods* hygienically, either home-made or com-mercially prepared baby foods in jars (heat these in the jar but do not put the lid in the microwave oven – cover with a piece of cling film).

Warm baby's bottle too, or his lotion, or his baby oil.

*Dry herbs.* Heat in the microwave oven until the herb will crumble between the fingers.

*Heat snacks* on toast. For example arrange baked beans or cheese on buttered toast and heat in the microwave oven.

*Make chutney* in minutes. Tomato chutney can be made in the microwave oven in 30 minutes. Follow manufacturer's instructions.

*Bottle fruit* in the jars. Follow manufacturer's instructions carefully. Use small jars. Make the syrup in the jar, heating the sugar and water in the microwave oven. Add the fruit and microwave-cook in the jar. The syrup becomes very hot so handle the jars with care. Do not put metal tops in the oven.

# Index